THE METAPHYSICAL SCIENCES OF THE BLACK GODS:
The Black Race Are The Extra-terrestrials
The Importance Of The Woman
The United States Bankruptcy And Your Birth Certificate

The Black Race Are The Extra-terrestrials
Chapter 1: The Spiritual Knowledge
Chapter 2 : The Metaphysics of Religion
Chapter 3 : We Are Spiritual Elements
Chapter 4 : Soul Is Frequency And Energy
Chapter 5: The Etheric Body & Melanin / Carbon
Chapter 6: The Vampire Recessives And The Melanin As Their Blood
Chapter 7: Light Carries Information

Earth Ran By Clones
Metaphysics **Of The Last Supper**

(Dialogue):
Contents Of The Light:
Papyrus 1: You Are Everywhere
Papyrus 2: We Are The Holy Books
Papyrus 3: The Zodiacs Is The Vibrational Energy To Melanin
Melanin, The Sun, And Your Health:
Melanin & The Brain:
Warning To Black Women:
Papyrus 4: Religion Has No God
Papyrus 5: The Science Of Sound

Christianity Decoded
Papyrus 1: The 12 Systems Of The Brain
Papyrus 2: What Is God
Papyrus 3: In The Image And Likeness Of God (Universe)
Papyrus 4: Melanin 666
Papyrus 5: The Soul Can Not Be Held
Papyrus 6: Light Gives Light

The Importance of The Woman
Chapter 1: Who is the Woman?
Chapter 2: Understanding the Woman.
Chapter 3: The Garden That Produces The Food.
Chapter 4: The Black Woman is Ma'at.

THE UNITED STATES BANKRUPTCY AND YOUR BIRTH CERTIFICATE
Chapter 1- The United States Is A Private Corporation
Chapter 2 - Your Birth Certificate Is A Contract
Chapter 3 - How To Defend Yourself In Court
Chapter 4 - Right To Travel Without Drivers License
Chapter 5 - Bar Association Does Not Qualify You To Practice Law In Court
Chapter 6 - Do Not Place Your Trust Or Faith In Man
Chapter 7 - HAARP (High Frequency Active Auroral Research Program)
Chapter 8 - The Secret Meeting On Jekyll Island
Chapter 9 - Government Controlled Churches
Chapter 10 - Truth About The Social Security Card
Chapter 11 - Queen Elizabeth And Social Security
Chapter 12 - IRS Is Not Part of The United States Governement
Chapter 13 - The U.S. Government
Chapter 14 - Rise of The Rothschilds / Illuminati
Chapter 15 - The U.S. Revolution
Chapter 16 - The Federal Reserve Act of 1913
Legal Defense And Definitons:

First and foremost I would like to give reverence to the Ancestors who gave us civilization to study so that we may be able to trace ourselves back to their existence and analyze the knowledge and wisdom that was embedded into the 3rd dimensional areas of this place that we call Earth, and once analyzed we may break it down and understand it and once understood, it may cause the elements within us and our DNA to shift or evolve us into the Extra-terrestrial Beings in whom we are. I would also like to bow and give honor and reverence to the Woman of the Universe for your superior work of bringing forth the Spiritual information through the triple darkness of your womb so that the Gods can come through because you got to remember that there would be no Gods without a Goddess.

THE BLACK RACE ARE THE EXTRA-TERRESTRIALS

PAPYRUS 1: The Spiritual Knowledge

The black man and woman have in their DNA the ability to understand the seen and the unseen. We have the capabilities to go outside of ourselves to a place where religion teaches you that you can only go if you are good here on Earth and this keeps us from being able to see our true purpose in this life that we are traveling upon. We are the Extra-terrestrials and what do I mean by that? Well lets not get spooked out because watching television has programmed us into thinking that an Alien or an Extra-terrestrial is some green monsters floating around in a spaceship. No it isn't. What is an Extra-terrestrial? Well we would have to use etymology in order to break this down into it's proper meaning. "Extra" means that you have something more than something or someone and "terrestrial" is one who is the inhabitant of where they geographically live and we are presently on Earth, therefore an Extra-terrestrial would be One who lives somewhere obtaining extra abilities or knowledge and wisdom that is Superior than most people that are in that geographical area. So why are we the Extra-terrestrials here on Earth? It is because we have in us an element that white people are putting into pills which you know as melanin, to keep them balanced with nature because they are not natural Beings, they are a processed people by way of an elemental scientific experiment called genetic engineering. Black people have this special type of melanin and this is what gives us color or complexion. This melanin is produced in the Pineal Gland which is also referred to as the third eye. Once the Sun touches this substance it responds back to us in a way that forces the Sun to give us energy and it keeps every cell in our body in a Cosmic Rhythm of 360 degrees of communication with other planets and things in nature. This is what makes us Phototrophic people because we convert Sunlight into energy. White people are "Heterotrophic people meaning that they can not convert Sunlight into energy due to the lack of the special type of melanin and that's why they are more healthier in dark, damp areas and this is also why they have to put on Sun block to block out the radiance of the information that only those with souls can retain or absorb. We are all Spiritual Beings with elements that are pre-encoded within our DNA, but we live on Earth, a 3rd dimensional realm which is ran by Souless Beings. These Souless Beings are known as the Caucasions, or the white race. These people are a hybrid species. They have no history nor have any of them experienced the crossing over into the 5th dimension. Why is that? Well the horizon of their thinking is incomprehensible beyond who they are. Number 1, anything voided of a soul is not natural nor can it go anywhere and exist with that which is natural unless it is on a 3rd dimension because the 3rd dimension is an illusional place where you can act and look natural but not necessarily Be natural and the 5th dimension has no illusions, it is the Creator of all things with soul and only that with soul can attain to its jurisdiction where it resides.

PAPYRUS 2: The Metaphysics of Religion

Religion. What is it? Again we have to use etymology to break it down so that we can interpret and understand its existence. The Re- in religion means something that has been or to do again. And religion is a cultural system and a way of living under beliefs and morals played under something created by man. So what is religion? Religion is something that has been copied from or has been done in a system in the past and is used as a way of culture under someone else or under another system to try to mirror what it has copied. And anything that has been copied is not the original it is only a reintroduction under someone else's system. Religion is not only a divisive mechanism among the people but the people who participate in it are one minded due to what their scriptures say when you read the bible it takes you away from being able to seek other knowledge because it is the God of that bible who says seek me and only me. This is a God that gives a character by the name of Moses 10 commandments in which one says thou shall not kill yet this God murders more people in the book than satan himself. Some people may say well that's because He is God and He can do anything. Ok. Well if this is the standard of morals that you set where you can create laws to say don't break them but you can break them yourself, it explains why Christians do what they do. There are more Christians in prison for murder and they justify it by saying well, "Ill ask for forgiveness and God will forgive me." Of course because you are following the same God that did the same thing you did so why even create laws if we are justified after we break them. God Murders (Passages to Refer to In Bible) Hosea 9:11-16 / Ezekiel 9:5-7 / Exodus 12:29-30 / Jeremiah 51:20-26 / Leviticus 26:21-22 / Isaiah 13:15-18 / Judges 15:14-15 / 1 Samuel 15:2-3 / Jeremiah 15:1-4 / Ezekiel 35:7-9. And then you have to also look at the contradictions in the bible. (Passages to Refer to In Bible) God is satisfied with his works Genesis 1:31 and then God is dissatisfied with his works Genesis 6:6 / God is never tired and never rests Isaiah 40:28 and God is tired and rests Exodus 31:17 / God is everywhere present and sees and knows all things Proverbs 15:3 Psalms 139:7-10 Job 34: 22,21/ God is not everywhere and does not see and know all things Genesis 11:5 Genesis 18: 20,21 Genesis 3:8 / God is the author of Evil Lamentations 3:38 Jeremiah 18:11 Isaiah 45:7 Amos 3:6 Ezekiel 20:25 / God is not the author of evil 1Corinthians 14:33 Deuteronomy 32:4 James 1:13. This is just a few but there are many more contradictories there in that book. Even before you open the bible it clearly states that it was translated out of its ORIGINAL version meaning that it is not original. When you go to the first book of the bible which is Genesis look at the word Genesis. If you take away the sis from the word it then becomes GENE. When you go to the schools of theology here in America they tell you that Adam (Atom) and Eve are a little over 60,000 years old yet the Pyramids in Egypt, Africa are over 132,000 years old. So who built the pyramids? Not only that but there is a European Anthropologist by the name of Professor Leaky who navigated the Earth to look for the Origin of the first people, he said he went into Europe and other so-called European countries and could not find any evidence of life, but when he reached Ethiopia, Africa he found the bones of a woman that is over 2 million years old yet Adam and Eve were only 60,000 years old. That is invalid and against the laws of time mathematics when calculating such a thing.

PAPYRUS 3: We Are Spiritual Elements

You are everything in the Universe. Wherever you reside is what you are. You reside on earth therefore you must study the elements of the earth because this is what you are, and when you study the elements and understand the elements of the earth you will be studying yourself to know who and what you are. Right now in 2015 as we say it is, the earth is wobbly. Why? Because there is a shift taking place in the Soular System which in turn is causing a shift in the Soul-ar System of those who have souls in this 3rd dimension. It is a few of Us Extra-terrestrials keeping it leveled due to the information and constant communication to the Constellation Systems in the Realms within the other galaxy's. If not for this the unconscious would cease to exist therefore making those who keep it afloat their Gods or Extraterrestrial Saviors. God does not exist, I just use it as a way of communicating with those who are conditioned in religion, the word God in its meaning and context that we use it today is only 500 years old and the world as a few know has no age which makes us ask what were we worshipping before that 500 year period. Someone asked me what should we be worshipping. Why worship anything is the question. What is it that animals worship? They don't read books or pray, yet they are in perfect harmony with nature and the Universe. That's because they survive off anything that is produced or manifested in the Universe. I said to him that we should worship everything and anything that sustains you or anything that sustains life. Water is the spiritual life bearer. Air is your defense against suffocation. Earth is your teacher of foundation. Fire is the Soul of your energy. When you combine these four elements it becomes Melanin which is the Seat of the Soul. These are the elements in which you should give reverence and honor to because this is what sustains your life. Doesn't your holy books tell you that God is the Sustainer? Well this is what you study and honor. Not a God that man made up for his own purposes and agenda's.

PAPYRUS 4: Soul Is Frequency And Energy
I speak the language of Spirits and Souls as I say again because this is what the unconscious understands. Soul and Spirit is nothing but frequency and energy. Every thought and everything in it is carbon and copper, and this equals up to energy. Everything is energy. There is no God but that which distributes all life which is Cosmic Rhythm of the Soular Systems. Every star is a Soul waiting to be manifested in a 3rd dimensional vehicle meaning a body. Like water it takes on it's higher and lower self. It exists no matter what. Whether hot or cold, it either freezes or evaporates. Whether it freezes or evaporates it still exists. It can never cease to exist. No matter its form. This plane or life that we live in is only an illusion. It doesn't exist. It only exist because you are contracted to something that is a part of it which is the body. We are not in male nor female form. We are in a vibrational form of the Universal substances. The Suns today are newborn. The binary Suns have been resting, now beginning to rise to make those without Souls extinct. Every thought is energy which can bring to life or manifest that which does not exist. On this planet earth you can bring to life that which is dead. All you have to do is speak Ones name. Whenever you speak you are using a life bearing frequency, the more sincere you are in speaking it the more closer you bring that One back to life.

PAPYRUS 5: The Etheric Body & Melanin/Carbon

The etheric body begins 3 inches beyond the body as a web of energy. It is our innermost layer, beginning at the spine which is the cells of the Earth's Solar System, and is also known as the pre-physical body. It is an electro-magnetic vibratory field that shields and energizes the dense physical body and integrates us with the Earth's energy fields. It fluctuates continuously in response to vibrational waves around it. The etheric body is known as the Soul. It is the Soul which is the womb that digests the unseen information which is frequency given by the Universe when it is vibrating at its highest frequency. When your physical body is shut down from sleep, the electricity in you flows at a straight calm rhythm to keep you connected to the 3rd dimension (Earth) while you may be somewhere unconsciously or consciously in tune with information that enters into your DNA by way of the Pineal Gland (Third Eye). This is why your melanin is produced more dominant while you are in presence of deep sleep. The Vampires(White Race) have knowledge of this and this is why they are inserting restless spirits (GMO- Genetically Modified Organisms) into the foods to keep your melanin supressed from being able to heal you. The Soul is nothing more than electricity or frequency which exists on a higher electro-magnetic magnitude of energy which gives a higher rhythm and a natural and healthier connection to its sustainers that you know of 4 which is (Air, Water, Earth, Fire), these four when put together is the ingredient of carbon which is melanin.

Melanin is what makes up or comprises the "Black Holes" throughout the Cosmo's. It being the cosmic substance which is dark matter, it is the essence of an infinite intelligence and the very fabric of space itself. Did you know that NASA uses a synthetic form of melanin to cover the entire under covering of the space shuttles when entering higher facilities of the Heaven's or the Universe? All of the wiring in these technological things are covered with melanin so that the heat that is generated from these objects being hurled into the atmosphere through the ionosphere can tolerate the heat and come out on the other side of space without exploding. That's why we as black people can tolerate the heat of the sun which uses this element melanin to convert sunlight into energy because we are phototrophic Beings. Just as natural plants has chlorophyll as their melanin which they use as photosynthesis to help convert sunlight to energy to grow. Melanin absorbs the heat and dissipates it. Actually allowing it to become a friction interaction when the combustion takes place. That's why we as black people are able to be at the center of the Earth at the Equator in pure intense heat temperatures of 110 degrees and our skin will not burn due to the melanin that is in tune with the unseen DNA of the Universe.

PAPYRUS 6: The Vampire Recessives And The Melanin As Their Blood

Melanin is the Universe in a microcosm, but it is in your body. Stop and think about that. AS ABOVE SO BELOW. It is a microcosm into outer space and when you look into a black hole you are looking at biological living light. Out of darkness comes light. It's in your so-called holy books. Melanin is black gold. This is why when you die (black people) they take out your organs, grind them down and dry them out to extract the melanin from your organs which in turn they make up melatonin pills out of your melanin to help them sleep but I've done research and found that many white people who are taking these melatonin pills are being attacked in their sleep by unseen forces. Do you know why? The dream world is the 5th Dimension because your 3rd Eye is activated by your melanin when you are asleep and by white people not having Soul's their frequency is not strong enough to cross all the way over into that 5th Dimension realm so when they take these melatonin pills they have hybridized the energy of the melanin which in turn causes them to have allergic reactions to our reality which is the dream world. The reason why you don't hear about these encounters by them in their news is because if they expose this, it will put them in an inferior state to those who are still unconscious and mentally asleep. Europeans whom I refer to as "Vampires" exist on a low frequency, meaning that they have no rhythm or Soul. Having Rhythm and Soul allows you to see and feel things on a Spiritual level. These vampires can only exist by way of your fear because fear is low frequency which I said before. Your blood is the "Spiritual Umbilical Cord" to the Soul. So when you deal with emotions such as fear, you produce an energy or an (ELF) Extremely Low Frequency that allows them to suck up your energy and this is what makes them appear to be like you. These are emotional people in the sense of how they exist. Emotions is their spirit and many of Us have adopted their ways in becoming emotional when at one time we were not emotional Beings but Spiritual Beings. So what has happened to the dominancy of Our spirituality? It is the "Emotional Systems" as I call them, such as religion, their Universities, and etc. Have you ever wondered why these actors such as Angelina Jolie and other cloned celebrities take interest in adopting children from African countries? They are raising these children to cross breed them with their own and to also extract their organs as business purposes. That's why when you get an identification card with the DMV (Department Of Motor Vehicles) they persuade you to become organ donors after you pass away from this realm. It is because your melanin is "Black Gold" and is worth millions of dollars and they take this from your organs, funeral home businesses has made billions upon trillions from selling body parts.

PAPYRUS 7: Light Carries Information

Everything that you see is light. Light is the source of telepathic information through frequency from one dimension to another. The real you can never die because it is your melanin which is Soul that captivates light to reproduce itself. The Universe has its own way of communicating. It chants and hums into your spiritual umbilical cord, so you are receiving information into your subconscious whether you know it or not. Whenever you sleep, the light within your pineal gland pulsates into a cosmic rhythm with the Universe. Every thought that enters into your mind is light before it manifests because light is the foundation to your every action whether you are utilizing your higher or lower self. Physical light could not exist without the spiritual light becoming the idea of its physical existence and you must understand that anything that has no Soul has no power to communicate with anything of light source beyond this realm. It is Us whom they use to be able to even taste the beauty of nature which we are and this is why they must keep studying Us because to study Us is to study nature.

Earth Ran By Clones

Jimmy Carter was the first U.S. President to be cloned. As you will read later on, it is important for world control that all the "leaders" be cloned, as they will then follow orders without thinking, and they have no emotions – no compassion, for instance, so they will carry out orders regardless of the moral implications of the action.

The mind is a liquid crystal so it can be downloaded into the new "clone." It frequently requires refreshing, and as time goes on, the frequency increases. That frequency will go down to every two weeks before it is time to discard that model and bring in a fresh one.

If you are observant, you will find differences in facial characteristics. When George Bush Sr was giving his speech in Tokyo, he collapsed and had to be removed. When he was brought back about ten minutes later, how many people noted that he had FRECKLES when brought back? Nobody in the press dared mentioned that.

He had been hit and killed by a Russian particle beam. On subsequent occasions a black box was seen positioned on both sides of him to counter these deadly weapons.

North of the border, Canadian Prime Minister Chrétien was known to speak out of the side of his mouth. One day he started speaking out of the OPPOSITE side of the mouth! Physicians will tell you that this is impossible. Of course, most of the time nobody really understood what he was saying, so nobody paid much attention to him at the best of times.

Russian Premier Gorbachev had a prominent scar on his forehead. That always remained, but you might recollect that he was "missing" for three weeks at one time, and the Russians had failed to concoct an adequate story to cover up that absence. This was the time when it took a full three weeks to create a new clone. A giveaway to those who understood.

To some this is a funny story. It was early days when President Jimmy Carter was cloned. Clones are programmed, and he was programmed to give a certain speech at the United Nations. To the dismay of the Americans, President Carter gave a speech opposing rather than supporting the topic in question. They hurriedly took him away for examination. It was later revealed that the Russians had 'ambushed' and re-programmed him with their version of what he should say.... talk about one-upmanship Security was increased.

The most important personages have THREE clones at any one time – in case there is an accident, such as happened in Tokyo. This also explains why there is such a huge entourage around the U.S. President – it is easier to hide the clones that way. Then a secondary clone can come out as if nothing had happened as in Tokyo.

The Obama that you see today in 2015 is not the same Obama that was running for presidential candidate in 2008. He had been assassinated way before his re-election but due to the cloning system he was restored back into the agenda of the political game. Representative Mcain when ran against Obama in the 2008 debates had passed before the final debate but was cloned in the midst of the run offs. Most of your celebrities are cloned and you walk around many who are considered to be agents.

Princess Diana understood clones and also knew that her life was in danger, for a number of reasons, so she agreed to be cloned while she herself was transported to the mountains of the Himalayas for safety. It was the clones who travelled in that fateful car in France, where the accident took place in the Pont de L'Alma tunnel in Paris, an ancient underground tunnel dedicated to Diana. She was actually murdered in the hospital where the surgeon reported that he had 'massaged her heart' .....

Before she died in 1997, Diana wrote a letter in which she claimed Prince Charles was planning to have her killed in a car crash "to make the path clear for him to marry (Camilla Parker-Bowles)".

The September 16, 1996, issue of U.S. News & World Report on page 22 has a "before" picture of President Clinton with a tumor on his neck, and an "after" picture of him after it was removed. If you pay attention to the photos, and notice the nose, ears, chin, eyes you can see that these are pictures of two different individuals. A controversy developed about this time when Bob Dole challenged Clinton to make his medical records public. Clinton is the only President, I am told, who has never made his medical records public. According to a filmed statement by Clinton's brother, Clinton is a cocaine addict.

(METAPHYSICS OF THE LAST SUPPER)

In Christianity Jesus is considered to be the Son of God. Let's take son and replace it with Sun. In the picture above you see the Sun of God surrounded by 12 disciples which is the 12 zodiacs. The Son is followed by the 12 disciples as also the Sun is followed by 12 zodiacs. The disciples in this picture are divided by four groups of three's. Each group represents the seasons or the 4 elements which is (Air, Water, Fire, And Earth).

"Remember that there is a difference between modern history and Ancient history. Modern history is more of a religion made up by the European illusion and Ancient history is what you see when you look up at the Sun."
Dr. Osei Kufuor

Dialogue: Just as your brain sends messages to your body to operate the certain body parts, well the food that you eat sends messages to different organs and cells and if the information that is transferred by your food is negative such as it being processed and genetically modified, these are negative frequencies transferred to these organs and cells which in turn tells these certain cells to attack different parts of the body such as the pancreas for example. It is the pancreas that regulates and produces the natural insulin carrying it into the bloodstream but when the negative information that is carried by light sends signals to the different cells it will attack causing the pancreas to become toxic and this is where diabetes sets in. The cells in your body consist of Nitrogen Particles so when it is lacking carbon which this helps those cells to breathe those Nitrogen Particles crack causing those cells to become cancer cells. Why? Because the information that is in your food transfers negative frequency waves into the body. We as black people have our own cure which is the melanin. We are considered Phototrophic Beings because we convert Sunlight into energy. The Sunlight transfers higher light frequencies of information to Us and the information causes the body to go into a hyperactive mode which is Our Nature. Parents (TAKE YOUR KIDS OFF OF THE RITALIN AND THE OTHER MEDICINES) this suppresses the melanin and slows down the Megahertz of their thinking. White people are considered Heterotrophs because they CAN NOT convert Sunlight into energy and this is why they have to put on sun block to block the Sun from skin cancer and anything dominant in Nature that doesn't respect you let you know that you are not Natural. Even plants convert Sunlight into energy by way of Photosynthesis because they hold an element similar to melanin which is chlorophyll.

Papyrus 1:
You Are Everywhere
The Europeans taught you that you had 5 senses, when all along you only have one. For an example, food has frequencies and this is how the information (nutrients) is transported through the body. So through tasting you can hear, and if you are eating foods that are processed, what happens is through your Spiritual ear of digestion it sends negative electromagnetic signals throughout the body causing chemical imbalances (mucus build-up) which initiates diabetes, cancer, HIV, and etc. Your eye's can hear whatever it see's and you can feel whatever you hear. This is how you Master the acceleration of the 3rd eye by deleting the dividing of the senses because whenever you put into your subconscious that your senses is divided then you yourself become a part of the illusion that causes the division. You are only a high frequency that has made a Soul contract with the dimension of being in the illusionary part of yourself (the body). The very thoughts in your mind are none other than something that is going on in another dimension or in the dreamworld which is the black man and womans reality. Europeans can never dream because the type of Christ in them which is the black dot or the Melanin is not present in them on a Spiritual level and this is the reason why they have pale skin meaning they lack the melanin which is the spiritual makeup of the Soul in Us. Europeans are not natural beings, and the only reason we think that they are like Us is because they are made up of a recessive spiritual substance which means they have an inferior type of melanin that has no bearing to nature. This is why they have to apply sunblock (block the Sun) and whenever anything of nature reacts to you in a negative reaction then you know that the

thing or person is not natural to its Being. The Earth itself has 1 sense that the have also divided which is the elements. Water is air. Air is fire. Fire is Earth. They are all 1 sense that makes up the Soul of the Universe. These elements is what sustains Us and even in your bible it states that God is the Sustainer which is the Universe. Well it also says in the bible that you are in the image and likeness of God, therefore you are in the image and likeness of the Universe meaning you are everywhere, whether you are in the form of a thought, a form of the elements or in the form of light which is information. Everytime you think a thought you are experiencing a part of yourself that is unseen. Day and night is a reflection of you, the illusion is the flesh, the reality is the dream. You only see yourself in one spot because you are focused on the flesh(the illusion), but the reality is that if you look all around you, you will be able to see yourself everywhere. Well we are a Spiritual people who was given religion, and when you mix spirituality with religion it is like creating something identical to yourself. You get an illusion that is over top of the reality. And what religion has done especially Christianity, is it has placed us in an illusionary mindset that has made us less independent on Nature which is common sense and more dependent on a man named Jesus who they call their savior yet, all over the world, there is more homeless children, young girls being raped, more wars and the sad part of this is, that these are all wars initiated by religion. And many of my religious brothers and sisters do not have a clue, that the church has more of a role in these wars than anybody else. And when this is presented to them they try to justify it by saying things like, well they are not us, but yes they are because you can not say that you are just the fruit on the tree and you are not a part of the roots, if these murderers (the Popes which is the catholic church, and when you do the historical research these people) are the roots, the beginners and the creators of Christianity so if you are a part of that body then you are also in the jurisdiction of their representation. This is why every year these popes and this so-called Queen Elizabeth tally up your taxes and split it amongst themselves. I don't want to go off the subject of what I'm here to speak about but we must understand what the foundation of the problem for black people is. It is religion. And it is because we have lost contact with the rhythm of our spirituality that connected Us to the heartbeat of the Universe. The subject I chose for today is Melanin And its Power In Black People. If you look around you, you will see and feel every part of yourself in the atmosphere. You are your thoughts and your thoughts are a manifestation of you. But what is melanin? What is this source Melanin is Soul and this is the Alchemical substance that makes Us as black people (black). It is your Soul and a Soul is none other than energy., It is a higher vibration of energy especially in black people because we hold all three types of melanin which is (Neuromelanin, Pheomelanin, and Eumelanin), . But it is also an information receiver and distributor. It captures and stores various forms of energy such as light, sound, and other senses that are unknown to this dimension. As this melanin comes into contact with sunlight, music, radio waves, cosmic rays etc. it absorbs these energies, stores these energies, and passes it to other cells of the body., So we as melanated people have the capabilities to charge up, or acquire energy without eating or drinking, but simply by being out in the sun , or in the presence of the right type of music and other forms of energy. This substance is the key to everything when it comes to Life.

Melanin in the ear vibrates on a Cosmic rhythm or frequency that connects you to other frequencies within the Universe. And all around you, you have what is called negative electro-magnetic waves which is known as (ELF's) extremely low frequencies, and you also have positive electro-magnetic waves. These frequencies are tuned in by Megahertz which is how the brain functions. Now Words also have frequency. Color has frequency. So what you say and how you say things can affect you and other people. That is why in Ancient times our Ancestors would chant in a certain way to bring forth healing and communications within the different Star systems and this is what the Dogons did. These were a group of people, our Ancestors who lived in the diaspora of Mali, West Africa around 3200 B.C. They were able to communicate and dialogue discovery of other extra-terrestrial Nature Beings within the Constellations. (Sirius A, Sirius B). Now you got to remember, that at that time there were no interruptions with the earth it was still on its normal journey, but today the earth is wobbling due to the unnatural beings (white people or what I call vampires) who is trying to process the atmospheric energies but since they have no souls, they can only understand the illusion which is the 3rd dimension because this is what they are. But how did the dogons do this. Well You have your physical eyes, and then you have your spiritual eyes. Your Spiritual eyes is your ears.(Now.) You may not know but, your ears is another part of the body that can see because not only is Melanin in the eyes, but it is in the ears. The Dogons understood this and they also understood that every body- part equaled up to one sense. Meaning you could sense through taste, sight, hearing and etc. They were able to put together these senses and pick up on certain vibrations. So what you look at and what you hear depending upon the frequency, you can also be healed or become

iii. Music for an example: Today the music that you are listening to, the frequencies have sped up tremendously since the late 80s and early 90s. Did you know that the music you listen to can intercept the nutrients from the food you eat? The foods that you eat, the nutrients contain frequency which goes into the blood because the blood is the entrance to the Soul. That is why in the bible it says that God heard their blood crying out from the grave. And we are going to get into that and break that down on a metaphysical level today also. But the nutrients in the food contains frequency that goes into the blood and if you are listening to music that is on a certain megahertz that is not condusive to your frequencies, I don't care how healthy you eat, the blood will not be able to intercept those nutrients. That's like taking a book of knowledge and flipping through the pages, you won't be able to get the knowledge because you are flipping the pages to fast and not only will you not be able to get the knowledge, you will not understand it. So the Cosmic Rhythm of the blood is moving so fast that, the food that you eat, your blood tosses the nutrients that it needs, because as I said food has frequency and also the food that you are eating today is processed or genetically modified, and anything that is processed or genetically modified is subsequently dead substance and this places you on dead frequency when you eat it causing diabetes, cancer and other ailments in the body, and that's why many with Our type of Melanin is sick. But we can go even further. The melanin as I said before is a receiver, and it is also a spiritual womb that digests information, so not only are we sick from what we eat physically, but we are in our condition because of the processed false information coming from religion and other imperialistic gadgets that we take into our spiritual womb which is the melanin. This is deep. Because you have living things within you, and it lives off of the information that you digest. A spiritual food and spiritual information is natural but man made religion is made up by man which makes it a processed mechanism of control. So if you are worshipping and taking religion into your Spiritual bosom you are digesting informational food that is processed and genetically modified. This melanin that we hold is very key because it is worth millions upon millions of dollars. And you must remember that anytime the government talk about studying DNA they are talking about how to alter and suppress the melanin which is you. There are cases where homeless people are so-called missing, but they are not missing. You have these FEMA agents that are coming out in the early morning between 3a.m. and 4a.m., especially in Georgia they've been doing this, they've been snatching these homeless people off of the street and taking them to secluded areas where there are laboratories underground. A few weeks later you look at the news and they are staging these suicide stories of people being found with missing organs when it is none other than those homeless people that they are snatching, taken to these laboratories and pulling the organs out of them for the melanin then they plant their bodies back on the street, because this is how they make their melatonin pills, and a lot of these white people take these melatonin pills to help them sleep. Also did you know that melanin is an alkaloid substance? Guess what else is an Alkaloid substance? Crack cocaine. And this is how they got us with the crack in the late 80s early 90s. Anytime you link the dominant chemical in a substance with the producer of that chemical it causes an addiction in that person, which is how they studied this melanin in Us and came up with the agenda to profit off of making us crack addicts. Back in 2013, I don't know if you remember the story of Kendrick Johnson, a 17 year old black brother in Georgia, who was found in a gym with his organs pulled out and he was stuffed with newspaper. Not only that but Trayvon Martin was also compromised suspiciously of his organs. And the same undertaker that tended to Trayvon Martins body was the same undertaker who tended to Kendrick Johnsons body. What a coincidence.

But our people are so caught up on racism when in actuality the war is bigger than that. This is more than bombs and missiles man . This is a Spiritual Warfare. This is a matrix that we are living in and all of this is an illusion and when you try to become liberated in a world that is an illusion, you become part of the illusion. When you look up at the Sun you are not really seeing its true Being. You are only seeing the shadow which is the physical part of it. The Sun is 93,000 miles away from the earth, and if you get within 1,000,000 miles within the Sun the natural characteristic of that Sun would be black. Why is that so? Because the Sun is made up of more than 50% melanin and this is the Soul of the Sun that sends or transcends the information through the light which is the shadow or the illusion. But the Melanin. What it is, it is something that helps you to receive or reflect that knowledge from other dimensions. (REFERENCE FROM DR. RICHARD KING BOOK A KEY TO FREEDOM PG 69 SAY, " THERE ARE MANY FORMS OF LIGHT THAT REACH THE SURFACE OF OUR PLANET SUCH AS MOONLIGHT, AND MANY DIFFERENT FORMS OF STARLIGHT, GALACTIC CENTER BLACK HOLES, NEUTRON STARS, RED GIANTS AND PULSARS. IT SAYS THERE IS ALSO AN ETERNAL INTERNAL SUN THAT SUPPORTS ALL DIMENSIONS OF ALL UNIVERSES).

Papyrus 2:
We Are The Holy Books

The whole bible is a book of science. Lets break down a small portion of Genesis. Genesis begins in darkness, the darkness represents the Dark Matter which makes up the Heaven and Earth (the body and Soul) and it is here that it is created in 7 days meaning the 7 systems of the earth (body) the 7 chakras. The word Genesis if you take away the (sis) becomes Gene (sis). A Gene is a part of the DNA that is used to identify a particular characteristic of someone or something and in Genesis one of the Systems is Jacob which is the Hip (the lower self). That is why when the man wrestling with Jacob lost the fight, he touched Jacobs hip. (Genesis 32:25) Jacob wins this fight with this man, which means he elevated from the hip (lower self) into his higher self (The Pineal Gland / 3rd Eye). In (Genesis 32:30) it says "So Jacob called the place Peniel, saying I saw the face of God meaning the (THIRD EYE OPEN). In the bible Lucifer is known as the Light Bringer and the Bright and Morning Star (Isaiah 14:12-14), in which the morning star rises at its highest horizon at 3 a.m meaning the melanin (Christ Energy) is being produced and rising on the 3rd day (3rd eye) the Pineal Gland. Christ is also refferred to as the Star in the East (Eastern Star / Female counterpart to the Masonic Order) (Matthews 2:2) meaning the light bringer, Christ and Satan is one in the same Christ the Sun rises (higher self) and Satan or Set, is the Sun that Sets meaning going down to Set (lower self) also Christ or the Christos is the melanin and Satan is the Mark Of The Beast the 3rd eye or the Pineal gland which also produces the melanin which is 666 and in melanin there is 6 protons 6 electrons 6 neutrons. This is the Power of Us which we reject in their churches and when we reject ourselves we fight that Soul within us which places Us on low frequency. When you operate on a 33 degrees of frequency you are dead, remember in the bible Christ died at age 33. In freemasonry you are told that the highest degree of the sciences is 33 degrees when that is not true. Water freezes at 32 degrees meaning that those sciences are not at its full capacity of being able to Master nature (nature of self). The masonry that is practiced today is boy scout. It is nothing compared to the Eastern Sytems of Freemasonry where it all started. Why do you think our muslim brothers and sistars face the East to pray? Because you are worshipping the black woman who is the Eastern Star and is also the black stone that you kiss in Mecca where you go every year. Kissing the black stone is a form of honoring the black womb. The black woman is the Master Mason who gave birth to its 720 degrees (720/ 7+ 2= 9) meaning the 9 etheric realms of science. We are the 9 ether that is formed within the 9 month gestation of birth from the Universe (the black womb). Every religious book and system is based on the "People Of The Sun" which is the melanated Beings that is known in the 3rd dimension or on Earth as the black people (Human Beings).). Just as I said before, the Sun, when you are looking at it from the place in which we are in, you are only looking at the illusion of it because you are wrapped up in an illusionary body, but the Soul within that Sun is the part that helps you to interact and interface with all of the Dimensions of the Universe. And the galactic black center holes that he is speaking of is none other than the melanin that is within the dimensions of the Pineal Gland which is the 3rd eye which represents the rising of the christos or the Christ, that's why it says that Christ rose on the third day. It was a metaphor, the melanin rising within the 3rd eye. The Christos, The Christ. And within the brain you have 12 systems that follows or reflects the 12 astrological zodiac signs. The 12 systems are the representation of the 12 disciples and this is the metaphysics of this here. There was no such thing as a Christ figure. These philosophers who wrote the bible, all they did was take everything in nature and made them people. You see, we rather believe in a White Jesus and somebody that we have never seen but you got millions upon millions of black people who died in a holocaust that were hung from trees and you want to worship 1 white man who hung from a dam cross whom you have never seen before. This is foolish. Your Ancestors gave you the remedy to heal yourself but the whiteman tells you not to go to Kemet. You say Jesus heals, well why is it that the majority of the world with diabetes, cancer, and all of these other ailments are religious people and you even got in your bible where it says do not eat of the swine but the major eaters of pork are in the church. And you can justify it by saying you can pray over it and all of that other bullshit but I can guarantee you, that if I put rat poison into your food, you can pray over it all day, but I guarantee you that you will die after eating it. All the praying that we do we should not be in the condition that we are in. The melanin is the key. It is all throughout the books of religion. In Isaiah it states, I will give you the treasures of darkness. Isaiah 45:3. Genesis in the bible begins in darkness, the darkness represents the Dark Matter (melanin) which makes up the Heaven and Earth (the body and Soul). Light comes out of darkness meaning Light represents Christ and Darkness represents Satan which is your higher and lower self. Lucifer in the bible is known as the Light Bringer and the Bright and Morning Star (Isaiah 14:12-14), in which the morning star rises at its highest horizon at 3 a.m meaning the melanin (Christ Energy) is being produced and rising on the 3rd day (3rd eye) the Pineal Gland. Christ is also refferred to in the bible as the Star in the East (Matthews 2:2 which is the (Eastern Star / Female counterpart to the Masonic Order) meaning the female and male is one in the same which is the masculine energy and the feminine energy. Christ and Satan is one in the same

Christ the Sun rises (higher self) and Satan or Set, is the Sun that Sets meaning going down to Set (lower self) also Christ or the Christos is the melanin and Satan is the Mark Of The Beast the 3rd eye or the Pineal gland which also produces the melanin which is 666 and in melanin there is 6 protons 6 electrons 6 neutrons. This is the Power of Us which we reject in their churches and when we reject ourselves we fight that Soul within us which places Us on low frequency. When you operate on a 33 level of frequency you are dead, remember in the bible Christ died at age 33. And what this says to me is that these people who follow this bible their knowledge is limited or frozen because water which is life freezes at 32 degrees. Now you all break that down.

Papyrus 3:
The Zodiacs Is The Vibrational Energy To Melanin
Mercurius is the ancient word for Mercury. Mercury is controlled by the God Tahuti. So when Mercury is in retrograde it is letting Us know as melanated Beings that we should focus our energy out of the illusion and meditate to control the different shifts that is going on at that time within the Universe which is yourself. It is a function of the zodiacal systems which is the vibrational information healer of Us. The 25th of December is when WE as melanated Beings are at our highest frequency, this represents the 13th zodiac known as Ophiuchus this is the Serpent wrapped around the cerebral cortex wrapped around the Spinal rising up the spinal cord (This zodiac symbol is on All medical vehicles / Ambulances) the serpent rising is the Kundalini energy rising into its Christos / Christ which is the 3rd eye because the serpent and the Christo or Christ is one in the same.THE Santa Clause is at the North Pole which is the Pineal Gland / 3rd Eye. He is known for sliding down the chimney which consists of black Sut (Set) which is carbon which is Melanin. He slides down the chimney to deliver presents which is a symbol of restoration, and when the presents is delivered, you rise in the morning to receive those presents meaning you have come into an awakening of self restoration (The Kundalini Energy). The Pope does the rituals that we are supposed to do at this time of year to intercept our energy while we stress over buying materialistic things that they make sure you can't afford and we keep these vampires alive by way of our fear and emotions. They need your blood

(emotions, fear etc.) to survive. Other than that they are nothing other than illusions. They can not do to you what you don't allow them to. Once the reality overcomes the illusion you will be able to access 100 % of your brain to do what you have to do to make these hybrid Europeans extinct out of your subconscious.

MELANIN, THE SUN, AND YOUR HEALTH

Light is something that is of extreme importance to us all since we are entering into the Age of Aquarius. This is when the earth in relationship to the sun and stars changes, it happens every 2000 years. The energy from the sun begins go back to the way it was when we were a great and powerful people. Many ancient writings and Holy books say this is the time that our Melanin is recharged, pineal glands decalcify, certain people will wake up and reinherit the earth. Some of us can feel it happening now.

The word "melanin" comes from the Greek word for black. Melanin is a unique biopolymer chemical that is in almost every organ in the body and in the skin of some. It is a pigment that is responsible for skin color, it ranges from yellow to blue black. One of its purposes is to shield us from the harmful radiation from the sun but its responsible for much more. In its purest form it is black. Its chemical structure does not allow any type of energy to escape once it comes in contact with it. Remember black absorbs energy and white reflects it. It is kind of like a battery that is always being charged up by the vibrations (energy) around it. Music charges the melanin centers much like the sun, deep bass sounds have longer wavelengths that fire up the human batteries. This is why Melanin Dominant (MD) people love bass and drums. Digital music CD's do not pass the natural odd harmonics of sound and sends fractured (negative) energy to our batteries. Better get out those cassettes and vinyl records they are analog. This is also true of microwaves, x-rays, electrical transformers, warring the watch on the left hand, tel-lie-vision, the alarm clock less than six feet from the head, just to name a few.

We now know MD people have different nutritional needs than melanin deficient people. MD people originated around the equator where the sun energy is strongest. There the minerals are more concentrated in the soil and there's more oxygen in the air because of the rich plant life. There plant based food is much more plentiful. Because of forced relocation, eating a northern flesh based diet, pollution, chemicals, legal and illegal drugs, digital music, alcohol, mis-eductation, mental and spiritual confusion the bodies melanin centers are out of balance and so are we. This effects personality traits, attitudes, health and every aspect of life. Most Melanin Dominant people are more right brained (emotional, creative, rhythmic, peaceful, respond better to pictures and symbols etc.). Melanin was thought of for many years by western science to be useless, I wonder why. Because Melanin is like a magnet it holds on to good and bad energy which affects its chemical structure positively or negatively.

When Melanin Dominate people Poison their bodies the Melanin holds on to these toxins more so than in Melanin-recessive individuals. Melanin is the reason Black people have a harder time getting off of drugs, alcohol, cigarettes, out of bad relationships, sugar (drug #1), processed foods, meats, milk products, junk food and breaking old habits. Black people are eating Caucasian people's food and it's proving to be deadly. It is very important to point out that people that originate around the equator must eat the food from that region that the creator put there for them. The polar bear and the grizzly bear can not eat the same food and survive even though they are both bears but their nutritional needs are different. When the chemical structure of Melanin is changed by negative energy and poisons these changes reduce the proper function of every organ of Melanin Dominate people, or the original HUE-MAN BEINGS.

This leads to:
Cancer
Heart disease
High blood pressure
Sleeplessness
Diabetes
Parasites
Hair loss
Impotence and frigidity
Bad attitudes
Fits of anger
Low energy and Laziness
Concentration and Memory problems
Hopelessness

And many of the problems the black people face today.

The solution is a change in attitude towards life, get lots of sun light, go out into nature as much as possible, change your diet to a plant based one, eat lots of organic green leafy vegetable and fruits, stay, away from negative people, negative situations, take herbs from around the Equator like Pau d' Arco, Cat's Claw, Black Seed, take only wholefood vegetarian supplements (like L-Phennylalanine a Melanin enhancing amino acid), take a vegetarian vitamin B6 complex, drink 64 oz. of filtered or spring water, use essential oils, use 100% vegetable oil soaps, practice Tai Chi Chuan, Yoga or get some type of regular exercise, find out more about your past, clean your colon and do a parasite cleanse, and Pray, meditate, and stay positive. Contrary to what we've been told all men and women are not created equal, there is and always will be color lines called Melanin. This incredible gift from the creator is a true path to greatness. Many people are out of balance with nature and nature gets rid of its mistakes. Each one has the power to change don't miss your calling light up your life. Who are you? Are you who you say you are? Are you doing everything you can to be who you say you are?

Melanin & The Brain
In the human brain are 12 centers of black melanin (12 Disciples). The pineal gland, the 3rd eye, or the Christ center which produces the 12 centers of black melanin is 1. Locus coeruleus 2. Substantia nigra 3. Brachialis 4. Paranigralis 5. Intracapularis subcerleus 6. Nervi trigeini 7. Mesencepahsius 8. Pontis centralis oratis 9. Tegmenti pedennculopontis 10. Parabrachialis 11. Medialis dorsomotor 12. Retro ambilgualis.
The most important is the locus coeruleus because when activated can cause you to coincide with the Universal light information and Astral project . You can buy "Yohimbine" to help keep it activate. It is a Central African tree bark. Also "Sacred Blue Lotus" is a great herb to assist in the activation of the Pineal Gland or the 3rd Eye (The Christos or the Christ). This was also an herb smoked by our Great Ancestors of Kemet and also used as a tea and perfume.

WARNING TO BLACK WOMEN!!!
If you are pregnant please avoid receiving an epidural. They will stick you with needles extracting the DNA of your unborn child to clone him/her then they place

the clone back into your womb, and you are unaware that you may be giving birth to a clone in which clones have no Souls. Be careful my beautiful black Women. Also do not allow the doctors to place any needles in you within 6 weeks of your pregnancy you produce a high count of Alkaloid from the melanin and this is what the hospitals sell to different countries like China and Japan to create crack cocaine. In the movie LUCY it is identified as CPH4 and they extract this from your amniotic sac during most check ups or within the time of pregnancy. I urge you not to do it.

Papyrus 4:
Religion Has No God
If you are following any kind of systems such as religion, following a god that creates commandments or laws that tells you thou shall not kill or steal then that very god turns around and kills and gives permission to other people to take land, then it would be understood why the people who follow that religion would do what they do such as kill and steal. Where is your god when babies in other countries are being killed by militaries of governments that are controlled by international banks and roman systems like the catholic church and the pope. Why is it that the highest carriers of diabete's, cancer, and high blood pressure are Christians, yet they pray over their food for that same god to bless it but you are dying. The question is what kind of power does your god have to the point where you can't even set up a church and speak about this god unless you go through the IRS to set up a 501c3 (non-profit organization / a business) to even use his name as a business for the agenda of the same people who pays for the weapons and finances the wars that you have seen happen in every nation in this world. This is why you religious people are dying, because you are worshipping something that they forced your ancestors who died to worship. Religion is the biggest business besides the prison system and the evidence has shown that your religion has no god and it has never shown any act within the historical foundations of the church or modern day Islam which both were used for imperialism. Your god tells you to love your enemy, yet that same god is the biggest influence towards its followers to not be of the devil. If the devil is an enemy then the laws should apply unless you are dealing with a double minded god, who it says by the way is a jealous god. Why would god have to be jealous of his own creation?

Papyrus 5:
The Science Of Sound

Sound is vibration and vibration is substance. It is all of the little drops of vibration that makes up the Sun. Sound can heal and it can cause disease because disease is nothing but low frequency that attacks the body from the substance of the information that enters into your being. For an example. When you heat up your food in the microwave did you know that the negative electromagnetic waves from the microwave produces vibrations within your food which causes a low frequency sound in the cells damaging the nitrogen particles creating cancer cells. Sound is also used to break up and disorganize matter. (Ultra-Sound breaks up kidney stones). There are sounds that are so low that you can not hear them, but they exist. There are sounds that are so high that you can not hear them, but they exist. There are vibrations around us that we can not see that we ignore and we only focus on the ones that we can identify that is acknowledged by the physical ear, but when we can lower the negative energies of our minds (by way of meditation or concentration), we can then focus on the vibrations or sounds that are in the outer dimensional circumference of our existence. When you are existing in a physical dimension (3rd Dimension) you are residing in an illusion (your physical body) that is turned out from other Beings or vibrational activities that is going on in the other dimensions. When the vibration within the melanin is in relationship to music frequencies on an 852 Hertz, this initiates Spiritual Order . When the vibration of the melanin is in relationship to music on a 528 Hertz, this endows you with the ability of DNA repair. (Beethoven and other philosophical musicians of art.) SO when you Listen to these types of music in the dark with the electrical outlets unplugged, this can help you go deeper into the dreamworld which is Our reality. (The dreamworld is Our Reality). You can get some blue lotus which is very effective in opening up the chakra's and other portals to get you to where you need to be. I smoke it all the time. Its called blue lotus. Most of the ancestors used this flower to open up different portals. And this flower gives reverence to Ra everyday. It opens up everyday at 8:00 a.m. and closes at 12 noon. This is a flower that can open up the melanin to help you receive the information around you.

Like I said, there is information all around you that is waiting to Travel through your DNA. It is carried by Light from the 3rd eye of the Universe which is the Soul(ar) System. This Light of information is being born every second and placed inside of the Stars to be released into the Christo's or the Christ who dwells within you, which is the Melanin.

CHRISTIANITY DECODED

PAPYRUS 1: The 12 Systems Of The Brain
In the human brain are the 12 centers of black melanin which in the bible you know as the 12 disciples. These 12 systems in the brain follows a dominant energy which is in the horizon(Heaven) of the brain called the Pineal Gland which is the gland that produces and crystalizes (Christ- a- lize) the element called melanin which is carbon. So if we take a good look at this system we can see that this is the way the story of Christ comes into existence these 12 systems (12 disiples) follows this carbon which is made up of light which carry's information into the 3rd eye which is "The Christ". This is the metaphysical story of the disciples following Christ. You have to understand that these so-called philosophers who translated this book took everything in nature and made them physical people. The Son of God is the Sun of God. The 12 disciples is the 12 zodiacs that follows the Sun. The cross that Christ dies on is the cardinal point that has four points which represents the four elements of the zodiac (water, air, earth, and fire), and these are also the elements that makes up the melanin. God is also reffered to being a Sun in Psalms 84:11. So if God is being referred to as the Sun then we must stop and analyze this, because it is in a book that is claimed to be holy, yet it has been translated many times. How can anything that is holy have mistakes to the point where it has to keep being transliterated over and over unless it is not what it is claiming to be. Why doesn't Christians do the history of the people who supposedly inspired this book called bible that was supposed to be given by god yet Christians can't give a description of what god looks like, sounds like, or even why he is reffered to being (He) instead of a she. When you hit many of them with the question all they say is that he is a spirit and he lives in the sky in heaven somewhere. That is insufficient. In the bible god sleeps, he talks, he walks in the garden, he murders and also create commandments that says thou shall not kill yet he murders more than anybody even satan himself in the bible. You must not be afraid to ask questions.

The 12 Systems Of The Brain:
1. Locus Coeruleus
2. Substantia Nigra

3. Brachialis
4. Paranigralis
5. Intracapularis Subcerleus
6. Nervi Trigeini
7. Mesencepahsius
8. Pontis Centralis Oratis
9. Tegmenti Pendennculopontis
10. Parabrachialis
11. Medial Dorsomotor
12. Retro Ambilgualis

PAPYRUS 2: What Is God
Every scholar of religion communicates on a level of who is god. Well it would be easier to ask the question of what is god, because then you would have to go outside of placing god in the jurisdiction of people. What is god? If god is the one who wakes you up everyday and prepare for you, this would be an act of sustaining, then we can very well say that god is the sustainer which also it states in your Christian books (Psalms 54:4). I can safely say that what sustains life on this realm is water, air, earth, and fire. The Sun has in it everything that you have in yourself , it sustains you emotional wise which spiritually connects you to who you are which is Soul. The water traps life and balances your thoughts therefore keeping your energy and frequency's hydrated. Air if it was to leave your illusion would cause you to become a part of that illusion making you non-existent. Earth keeps you foundated and leveld with the Constellations helping you to balance rhythm and reaching dimensional destinations. Many Christians say that sun worship is satanic but if the sun was to leave the earth, everything would cease to exist. That's all Christianity is. They are unconsciously sun worshippers which is a great thing but not in the aspect in which they are worshipping it. What is the day set for all of your energy and money to be directed to a thief in the pulpit? (Sun-day). If the money you are giving to the church is supposedly given to god then you must ask what is gods account and routing number? What does god even need money for if he is your sustainer? It seems that someone else is being sustained and it is not god.

Papyrus 3: In The Image And Likeness Of God

In genesis 1:27 it states that god created man and woman in his image and after his own likeness. Well we have just established that god is everything in the Universe, so if god created us in his image and likeness then we must be in the image of the Universe and like the Universe. The Universe is made up of dark matter (melanin) and atoms that consist of electrons, protons, and neutrons. Guess what? We are made up of these very same elements thus making us look like and act like the Universe. Now I see why god is characterized as being human in the bible because you and I are one with the Universe also making the Universe a human. This is a mirror image of two dominant forces being of the same elements and acts of law within the same existence. So if you study the Universe you are studying yourself and when you study yourself you are studying that which is under the illusion that we call flesh which you are not a part of. That's why in your bible it says be not of the flesh, John 1:13. So even your Christian books tell you that but it is the understanding that is missing placing you into a carnal mind which is nothing other than the matrix. Everything inside of you is going on outside of you. The stars are in cosmic rhythm with the body of the Universe as your cells is in cosmic rhythm with your body which is the Universe. There is a new Universe being born in the Original Man and Woman who are one in the same, a Universal birth of Souls coming through the Constellations or the Woman, and that's why in Revelations 12:1-3, the Woman giving birth meaning a energy is being born which is the Christ energy that will carry those with that Soul DNA (Melanin) into the 5th dimension which is the opening of the Pineal Gland or 3rd eye which produces the melanin. This is causing everything of hybrid species to go into extinction and this is known by those who you know as the Pope's and in their catacombs they have the prophecies of this from our Ancestors from Kemet. This is why they are killing all of the black youth, but what they don't know is that the more of us they kill the more of us they are freeing.

Papyrus 4: Melanin 666

The reason why these vampires (Europeans) in their Christian literature make claim that the mark of the beast is 666 is because within melanin which makes us black people is (6 protons, 6 electrons, and 6 neutrons) which also represents the Christ energy. You have to metaphysically understand what Christ dying on the cross for your sins mean. If a sin is a debt, a debt is an illness which is the flesh that wraps around you which is the Soul. Whenever you are in oppression by your flesh by illnesses it is melanin that is the healer or the defense against whatever is trying to attack that which is consuming the knowledge and wisdom , the spiritual womb called the 3rd eye, which is the Christos or the Christ energy. This is what is called paying for your sins. Religion teaches you to hate yourself by making a part of yourself to appear evil. They say that the mark of the beast is an evil being, it is looked at as being dark and evil, so when you start to believe this without really decoding or understanding it , you start to hate what you don't understand and if you are hating something that is spiritually a part of you unconsciously then you are turning a force against yourself by way of your thought manifestations of what you are putting in your mind and that places you on a low frequency which can cause illnesses and chaos within yourself. 666 is you and it is what connects you to nature because nature also produces 666 in the Soular System as you also produce. As above so below.

Papyrus 5: The Soul Can Not Be Held
A Soul can not be held as water can not be held. The water even though when frozen is the Soul of the ice, the water can't be held it will eventually melt and become water again it can not be held, as we (the Soul) is in the body of the flesh we can not be held. The Soul is frequency and frequency is energy. Everything around you in nature has a Soul which makes you everything around you. The black race is rhythm, we are the thoughts that enter the minds of our own minds. Until we put into our minds that what we see physically on this planet earth don't exist we will not exist and you will be giving energy to the vampires who are without Souls and as long as you give them that energy they will be able to control the mind that you feed them the energy from. They will hang your Christ energy on the cross(Stress, depression, cancer, etc.) and your spiritual eye will not be able to open to heal or carry you over into the heavens of the Constellations (5th dimension).

Papyrus 6: Light Gives Light To Understanding
You have always heard people say, "Shine your light." What exactly does that mean? Well what is light? Light is the natural agent that stimulates sight and makes things visible. So whenever you shine your light you are speaking

something from an agent, which is your heart that directs your mind in saying something out of your mouth to make something visible to whomever you are shining light upon. Light also gives motion. Wisdom is something that is very identical to light. Why do I say that? I say this because if a person who has a mind that is dark, dark meaning that if the mind is dark it is without motion and when you speak wisdom to that mind, it starts to create a light within that person which will bring motion into his or her mind. Light gives light to understanding. In order for you to have understanding, you would have to have the knowledge to understand the understanding itself. If you are traveling on your journey(life), you could be walking in darkness and be alright with it, but when you start to put a light in your travel it helps you to understand the road much better, because in darkness you are traveling but you don't know where you are traveling. That is like speaking without thinking which is dangerous, but when you have light in your mind you will not just be saying something just to be saying it, you will get permission from that agent which is your heart before you say it and this would be an example of you shining your light. So in your travel you are a builder with wisdom meaning light, in which light also travels at the rate of 186,000 miles per second. So if you become that light then that will be the rate of your speed within your journey. I am your brother and by the time I'm finished with you the black man and woman you will be once again the master of builders as you once were of civilization.
Emotion is energy. Religion uses that energy to devour you by making you direct that energy toward a pulpit where oppression strains over your emotions.

The battlefield is to be fought in the dreamland, because when those with melanin (Souls) sleep they go into their true selves. The real world is inside of you. Everything outside of you is an illusion.

THE IMPORTANCE OF THE WOMAN

Chapter 1
Who is the Woman?

The woman is a very distinct power within the Universe. As a matter of fact, the Universe and the woman both have something in common that man does not have. They both nuture the creation and life within themselves. They both give life and have everything in them to nurture the life that they produce without having to depend on anything outside of themselves. The woman is a very distinct figure with a source of power that ignites the strength of the man. Even though both were created for one another and they both compliment one another, it is something that the woman carries mentally, morally, and spiritually that man can only attain through stages whereas he has to keep falling in order to see and accept most of the things that the woman already has knowledge of when she enters into Gods Universe. What I am saying to you is that the woman comes into the world fully developed mind wise, with the tools to build the man in a way that he can not build himself. But in order for her to build him, he has to provide her with something of a spiritual, mental, and moral respect that will get him to the stages of knowing his true purpose to her. I will take you to the door of how to do it brothers, but you have to be willing to walk through. Having all of these recognitions in a woman does not make you less of a man, it makes you more of a man that you can humble yourself and bow and give way to the divine feminine. It makes you a divine masculine to give reverence to the woman. The woman is a world within herself. So without the presence of her in your life you would have no world to live in. Today she is not respected in terms of being uplifted and protected, especially the black woman. The blackwoman is a very distinct creation of God and also a very distinct creator of man, from her genetics all the way to her nature. As the Honoarble Elijah Muhammad says, she is the first teacher and the mother of civilization, therefore when the teacher is disfigured the students is disfigured, and when the mother is not protected, then the children will be the hostage of an environment that has a lack of moral values to humanity. This subject is dedicated to the women, so brothers if you can't bare to hear a word that will help you to uplift the woman, which is your Heaven, then you will forever be in Hell. I'm just warning you of what is to come if you do not listen to what I am saying to you today. I am a man from God with the duty of warning my people, the black man and woman of what is to come. But to save a people we must save the one who gives birth to the people and I say nomore to disrespecting the black woman. Nomore! For you brothers who will continue to go along after today abusing and misusing the woman, you will pay with your life, this is not a threat from me, but from He who created me. You can make mockery of me all you want, but remember these words that I am about to give you and let them be a guide for you to uplift your woman. May Almighty God bless you my brothers and sisters and find favor in you for you are the chosen people of God. The Importance of the Woman!

Chapter 2
Understanding The Woman

The woman is like wisdom. She has a radiation of knowledge from head to toe if you can understand the wisdom in her Universe. You have to understand that the woman is the wisdom of the Earth. Brothers you can look at her and see the beauty of her wisdom physically all you want, but you will never be able to understand that wisdom until you understand her importance. A man can have all the knowledge in the world, but if you do not understand the knowledge that you have then you will be lost in the world that you get it from, and this is like the woman if you do not understand her then you will be lost with the knowledge that you have for her when you are present in her. How do you understand the woman? There are three things in the Universe that keeps the Universe afloat and balanced, these three things are the sun(heart), moon(mind), and the stars(feelings). The woman has very distinct moral values apart from any other being in this world that radiates beautifully internally, which brings about external sunshine of respect and she is more adapt to bring this about whenever her heart is in a state of balance and peace. The woman is a Universe and she has a heart which is like the sun because whatever she touches from that part of herself, if she is balanced and protected she will bring about a civilization(planets) that will revolve around her with a circle of respect that you plant in her to create that civilization. Most importantly, you must pay attention to her mind(moon), which is her moon. Why the moon? Because the moon is what moves the waters and water represents life and knowledge. Her mind is what creates the mindstate in the life that is within herself, so whatever knowledge she obtains goes into the

fetus as it grows, her mind is like the moon that moves the knowledge into the life which is inside of herself.The womans whole body is made up of 90% stars which is the feelings to the Universe. One wrong move in understanding these stars in her Universe will cause the planets(civilization) to collide against one another. This is what is happening today. The woman is abused so therefore our children(planets) are growing up colliding one against the other causing the Universe to be unbalanced. If the brothers will just listen to me today, we must take orbit into our Universe(woman) and feed the proper wisdom to the planets and stars (civilization, children) to bring about a better generation of us to prepare the black man and woman for the rule of the Hereafter that God has promised us that He will take the last and make them
first(Us), and take the rejected stones that the builder rejected(Us) and make them the head stone of the corner(Us). This is our future, but God will not move us any further until the most important tool of our civilization builder is protected and respected. The Woman.

Chapter 3
The Garden That Produces The food

The Seed That Produces The Food When planting a seed to produce food, one must find a good ground of soil to plant that seed which will bring forth the product. When you are growing good vegetables you need water and light to help the soil give motion to the seed that is being planted in the soil. The woman is very similar in this way of producing the seed that she carries. The seed or life that is in her needs water(wisdom) and light(knowledge) but most importantly good soil(understanding) when carrying a product in the womb. When the woman is carrying life(seed) in the womb, whatever is done on the outside affects that life inside of the womb. As men we must do all that we can to make sure that our producer is protected from the negative thoughts and actions of this world. Satan is setting traps daily to keep you away from your woman so that your seed will grow up out of the garden without respect for the garden that produced it. If you look around today, mothers are raising children on their own and because the man is not present the masculinity of the mans wisdom can not take affect on the unshaped mind of the seed that is growing. The light and the water is the wisdom and knowledge that the man must instill into the woman to shed light on the seed inside of her. She is the garden and he is the gardener. Once the woman is being respected by the man, receiving that love from him helping to put her at ease, then the seed within that garden will have understanding, and in having understanding that seed will grow up out of the garden healthy and beautiful to the garden and the gardener that produced it. Do not beat the woman! Beating the woman is like beating yourself. If the woman is down, civilization will have no meaning to humanity. Stop calling her outside of her name brothers. She will soon turn bitter against you and that will be like committing suicide because once the woman loses respect for you brother, your heaven will be of nomore existence, you will be living in hell due to the way you have shaped her. The woman is the producer of civilization. If you take all of the women out of the world, who would be around to produce the fruit that is needed to bring about the existence of humanity? Yes you can say that men is needed to plant the seed, but remember that the woman has very distinct DNA that can carry her on forever that a male does not have. She is like the sun and the man is like the planets. The sun can stand by itself but if the sun goes out then the planets will collide. I'm your warner and everything that I say to you, if you take heed to what I am saying, you will be able to bring the woman back into the favor of respect for you brothers. The black woman is beautiful. Stop running to the white woman for acceptance of the white man and his wealth. His wealth has passed away like wildflowers and the white race itself shall soon pass away. As the bible says, "Go into your own kind." Black man your woman is the most beautifullest woman on the earth. Stop trying to race mix. They are only using you to keep their race alive. Can't you see that God is getting rid of them as the bible says" The devil came, but for only a short time". Not to say that all women should not be respected but how can you respect any other culture of woman if you can't respect your own. Respect your own first.

Chapter 4
The Woman Is Ma'at

Everything in creation is brought forth by the woman. The woman is the creator of science and all of the architects of the world. Look at the name woman. Take away the (womb) and the word becomes (man). That is because she is the completed human being. the man is just a degenerate from the woman who created him in her image and after her own likeness. The woman has a strong DNA that dates back to her Goddess times of Egypt where her connection to her sister the Goddess Ma'at still is alive within the blackwoman today. Who is Ma'at? Maat literally means Truth in Egyptian. In Ancient Egypt, Maat was not just a Goddess, but was a concept as well. The Goddess Maat was that which kept balance and order in the entire Universe! Not just the people of Egypt (Kemet), but everything in the heavens and the earth bowed down to the rules of Maat. She was what controlled the seasons, she controlled the water flowing in the oceans, and she controlled the circle of life among the animals. She controlled life and death, and all that was. And she kept it all in balance. The story of Maat starts at the beginning of creation. Because of the Goddess Maat being both a Goddess of truth and justice, and a concept of balance and order, she was the main icon of Judges and Courts. In Egypt, the judges would wear a feather on their heads, and most of them were also priests of Maat. The courts were often temples to Maat. Because of this, when the Greek culture took over power, they used the word Logos for Maat. Logos was what they used to judge a persons life. In the bible, Logos was used instead of (Word), which was also another name for Jesus. John 1.1: In the beginning was the logos*, and the logos* was with God and the logos* was God. The representation of the Goddess Maat was that of a teenage, winged girl. Sometimes also depicted as twin girls. She always wears the Ostrich plume on her head, and hold the scales in her hand when weighing the hearts of the dead. She is wife to either Anubis or Thoth, and has no children of her own. She is a Goddess of the Autumn Equinox, when day and night are of equal length, and when the seasons are in the waning. Her name literally means Truth, and she is the Goddess of truth, justice, balance and order. She is the Goddess for Libras. She is the Goddess Themis in Greece and the Goddess Tiamat in Babylonia. She is neither good nor evil, because nature needs both to exist, she is neutral. Notice how today there are more storms and earthquakes going on in the world. This is because the energy of the woman is unbalanced due to the disrespect of the life she creates. The black woman has power that connects all of them as one to Ma'at which gives them the strength that causes these storms and catastraphes under the condition in which they are in. Brothers we have to stand up or we are out of luck with the credibility of our creator. Satans goal is to turn us against the woman but it would be foolish to fall into such a trap that you will have to suffer for later. The woman is Ma'at!

The United States Bankruptcy And Your Birth Certificate

"The real truth of the matter is, as you and I know, that a financial element in the large centers has owned the government of the U.S. since the days of Andrew Jackson."
Franklin D. Roosevelt, U.S. President,
In a letter written Nov. 21, 1933 to Colonel E. Mandell House.

Heaven To Me
Heaven to me, when my weakness is at its highest strength, and my mistakes is at its highest victory, God is at my highest interest because I am in the image and likeness of Him. He is Heaven to me

CHAPTER 1
The United States Is A Private Corporation

Did you know that the United States is not a country? It is a private corporation that was set up as a surety holding insurance company to collect taxes from it's citizens to pay off the National debt of 1933, in which bankruptcy, which was filed by President Roosevelt in 1933, and through the birth certificate citizens became the surety or collateral for the U.S. debt.. We will get to IRS and taxes later, but for now I'm going to show you how these private coporations such as the Treasury Dept., the New York Stock Exchange, ALL hospitals and the Vital Statistics are all connected, but first I will give to you below the bankruptcy initiation act given by congress to sell american citizens to private bankers by way of the birth certificate. This is Speaker Representative James Traficant Jr. of Ohio addressing the House of representatives on behalf of the United States March 9, 1933; It Reads [Speaker- Rep. James Traficant, Jr. (Ohio) addressing the House: "Mr. Speaker, we are here now in chapter 11.. Members of Congress are official trustees presiding over the greatest reorganization of any Bankrupt entity in world history, the U.S. Government. We are setting forth hopefully, a blueprint for our future. There are some who say it is a coroner's report that will lead to our demise. It is an established fact that the United States Federal Government has been dissolved by the Emergency Banking Act, March 9, 1933, 48

Stat. 1, Public Law 89-719; declared by President Roosevelt, being bankrupt and insolvent. H.J.R. 192, 73rd Congress m session June 5, 1933 - Joint Resolution To Suspend The Gold Standard and Abrogate The Gold Clause dissolved the Sovereign Authority of the United States and the official capacities of all United States Governmental Offices, Officers, and Departments and is further evidence that the United States Federal Government exists today in name only. The receivers of the United States Bankruptcy are the International Bankers, via the United Nations, the World Bank and the International Monetary Fund. All United States Offices, Officials, and Departments are now operating within a de facto status in name only under Emergency War Powers. With the Constitutional Republican form of Government now dissolved, the receivers of the Bankruptcy have adopted a new form of government for the United States. This new form of government is known as a Democracy, being an established Socialist/Communist order under a new governor for America. This act was instituted and established by transferring and/or placing the Office of the Secretary of Treasury to that of the Governor of the International Monetary Fund. Public Law 94-564, page 8, Section H.R. 13955 reads in part: "The U.S. Secretary of Treasury receives no compensation for representing the United States?'

Gold and silver were such a powerful money during the founding of the united states of America, that the founding fathers declared that only gold or silver coins can be "money" in America. Since gold and silver coinage were heavy and inconvenient for a lot of transactions, they were stored in banks and a claim check was issued as a money substitute. People traded their coupons as money, or "currency." Currency is not money, but a money substitute. Redeemable currency must promise to pay a dollar equivalent in gold or silver money. Federal Reserve Notes (FRNs) make no such promises, and are not "money." A Federal Reserve Note is a debt obligation of the federal United States government, not "money?' The federal United States government and the U.S. Congress were not and have never been authorized by the Constitution for the united states of America to issue currency of any kind, but only lawful money, -gold and silver coin.

It is essential that we comprehend the distinction between real money and paper money substitute. One cannot get rich by accumulating money substitutes, one can only get deeper into debt. We the People no longer have any "money." Most Americans have not been paid any "money" for a very long time, perhaps not in their entire life. Now do you comprehend why you feel broke? Now, do you understand why you are "bankrupt," along with the rest of the country? [End]

Now lets connect all of this to taxes. In Article 1 Section 8 of the Constitution it clearly states that ONLY congress has the power to lay and collect taxes for the sole purpose of paying off the United States National debt. This alone kills two birds with one stone. Number one, the constitution admits that your taxes helps to pay off their National debt. Number two, if only congress is given power to collect taxes, why is the IRS collecting your taxes, and the IRS is not even a part of the government. Thats right. It is a private corporation incorporated in Deleware on July 12th 1933 as a for profit by three Natzi's by the name of Clifton Barton, Ellen Barton, and Lawrence Echevarria. Is it a coincidence that all of this is happening in 1933, the United States files for bankruptcy, the Internal Revenue Service is set up and then here goes the birth certificate, which contracts the citizens forcing them to pay taxes at a later date due to your parents signing you over to the state by way of the birth certificate. All the taxes that you pay DOES NOT go to the United States Treasury because it does not exist. The treasury department of the IRS is the treasury of the Popes of Rome under the Treaty of Rome, and not one penny goes to schools, social security, etc. Your taxes are divided amongst the Queen of England and the Popes of Rome.

Income Taxes are for Federal Employees to pay. A 'Federal Citizen' is one who works for the United States of America. The United States of America is a corporation and if one is a citizen of it, they are a corporate person citizen, and must pay taxes - Not the natural person of which all federal employees / public servants work for the purpose of upholding and preserving the unalienable rights of the natural person. They are Trustees with a derived authority (Constituion). The articles within the Constitution describe their duties and obligations as Trustees. The Constitution is the Law of the land, and if natural people do not want to be molested they must enforce the constitution and be sure it is not violated against them. This is the already established law and there is no other Law in this land. There exist "color-of-Law" which is negative law as opposed to positive law. "Considering that senior officials at the Internal Revenue Service are fully aware of the fact that there is no law currently in existence making a U.S. citizen liable for or required to pay either the income tax or the social security employment tax, only a truly generous citizen would, upon discovering this, continue to voluntarily donate these taxes to the government by allowing them to be withheld from his paycheck on a 100% voluntary W-4 withholding agreement. But, then again, the IRS would be dead in the water without the voluntary (and docile) compliance of employers and employees and has said so all along." -- William Cash, IRS Senior Manager.

Franklin D. Roosevelt - Executive Order 6073 - Reopening Banks (1933)
By Virtue of the authority vested in me by Section 5 (b) of the Act of October 6, 1917 (40 Stat. L., 411), as amended by the Act of March 9, 1933, and by Section 4 of the said Act of March 9, 1933, and by virtue of all other authority vested in me, I hereby issue the following executive order. The Secretary of the Treasury is authorized and empowered under such regulations as he may prescribe to permit any member bank of the Federal Reserve System and any other banking institution organized under the laws of the United States, to perform any or all of their usual banking functions, except as otherwise prohibited. The appropriate authority having immediate supervision of banking institutions in each State or any place subject to the jurisdiction of the United States is authorized and empowered under such regulations as such authority may prescribe to permit any banking institution in such State or place, other than banking institutions covered by the foregoing paragraph, to perform any or all of their usual banking functions, except as otherwise prohibited. All banks which are members of the Federal Reserve System,desiring to reopen for the performance of all usual and normal banking functions, except as otherwise prohibited, shall apply for a license therefor to the Secretary of the Treasury. Such application shall be filed immediately through the Federal Reserve Banks. The Federal Reserve Bank shall then transmit such applications to the Secretary of the Treasury. Licenses will be issued by the Federal Reserve Bank upon approval of the Secretary of the Treasury. The Federal Reserve Banks are hereby designated as agents of the Secretary of the Treasury for the receiving of application and the issuance of licenses in his behalf and upon his instructions. Until further order, no individual, partnership, association, or corporation, including any banking institution, shall export or otherwise remove or permit to be withdrawn from the United States or any place subject to the jurisdiction thereof any gold coin, gold bullion, or gold certificates, except in accordance with regulations prescribed by or under license issued by the Secretary of the Treasury.

No permission to any banking institution to perform any banking functions shall authorize such institution to pay out any gold coin, gold bullion or gold certificates except as authorized by the Secretary of the Treasury, nor to allow withdrawal of any currency for hoarding, nor to engage in any transaction in foreign exchange except such as may be undertaken for legitimate and normal business requirements, for reasonable traveling and other personal requirements, and for the fulfillment of contracts entered into prior to March 6, 1933. Every Federal Reserve Bank is authorized and instructed to keep itself currently informed as to transactions in foreign exchange entered into or consummated within its district and shall report to the Secretary of the Treasury all transactions in foreign exchange which are prohibited. Citation: Franklin D. Roosevelt: "Executive Order 6073 - Reopening Banks," March 10, 1933.

CHAPTER 2
Your Birth Certificate Is A Contract

From the time that you are born in the United States you are issued a birth certificate which identifies you as state property, which gives jurisdiction to America over you as a person. On your birth certificate there are red numbers and those numbers are set up in the United States Treasury as your stock number whichis then sent to the New York Stock Exchange to have you recorded as stock. This certificate is then sold to the international bankers as collateral for the debt of the United States. Each one of us, including our children, are considered assets of the bankrupt United States which acts as the "Debtor in Possession.When a child is born, the hospital generally sends the original, not a copy, of this record of live birth to the State Bureau of Vital Statistics, sometimes called the Department of Health and Rehabilitative Services (HRS). Each STATE is required to supply the corporate UNITED STATES with birth, death, and health statistics. The STATE agency that receives the original record of live birth keeps it and then issues another Birth Certificate in a different form where the name of the baby is spelled in ALL CAPITAL LETTERS. This creates a 'legal person' as opposed to a natural individual. The Birth Certificate issued by the State is then registered with the U.S. Department of Commerce – - the Executive Office – specifically through their own sub-agency, the U.S. Census Bureau, which is responsible to register vital statistics from all the states. Thus, the birth certificate is registered in international commerce. The word registered, as it is used in commercial law, does not mean that the ALL CAPITAL version of the name was "merely" noted or recorded in a book for future reference purposes. When a birth certificate is registered with the U.S. Department of Commerce, the Treasury will issue a bond on the value of the birth certification. That bond is then made available for purchase on a securities exchange and is bought by the Federal Reserve Bank. This purchase then become the authority or collateral to issue Federal Reserve Notes, which we use as a medium of exchange. The value of the bond in today's world is $630,000. The bond is then held in trust for the Federal Reserve at the Depository Trust Corporation at 55 Water Street in New York City, about two blocks down the street from the Federal Reserve. It is a high-rise office building and the sign in front reads: "The Tower of Power." " We are designated by this government as human "resources" or human "capital". You may have noticed that all "personnel" offices have been converted to "human resource" offices. The government assumes the role of the Trustee while the newborn child becomes the beneficiary of his own trust. Everything the child will ever own is vested in the government. The government then places the Trust into the hands of the parents, who are made the "guardians." The child may reside in the hands of the guardians until such time as the state claims that the parents are no longer capable to serve in which they hire another private corporation called the Department of Social Services or DSS to kidnap your child when they deem you are unfit as a parent but little do we know that in international courts you can bring kidnapping charges against these corporations. The state then goes into the home and removes the "trust" from the guardians, because when you sign that birth certificate your child became a TRUST to help pay off their National debt. Notice that the name on the birth certificate is in all capital letters? This is called a strawman name. It is not a real person. That is not your name on that birth certificate, because only corporations and businesses are in all capital letters. So for example if the court send you a summons and your name is in all capital letters on that summons and you agree that it is you, then you have given that court authority and jurisdiction over you to adjudicate you or prosecute you illegally. Anything that is in all capital letters is not real. Say for example if you set up a checking account with Bank of America and you go into debt with Bank of America and creditors start calling and harrassing you, remember that you did not sign a contract with the creditors, therefore you say to them to send the contract stating that you owe them and to present to you the original copy of the contract with them and demand the original disclosure documentations, because you did not contract with them you contracted with Bank of America. The creditors then sends you a letter with your name in all capital letters saying that you owe them, remember that a name in all caps is not real it is a corporation and you are not a corporation, just return that letter to them as a return to sender because the name in all capital letters is not you. When a child is born within the corporate United States, a Record of Live Birth form (a commercial Bill of Lading), or similar, is issued by the hospital. The father and mother sign this hospital form (a receipt for goods) as the parents (manufacturer) and title holders (owners) of the goods (child). The transfer of the property Rights (the child's Rights) to the State is accepted by the signature of their government agent, a State licensed Physician. The parents have unknowingly pledged their child's future and labors to the government and signed a presumed contract. This converts the legal status of their child to that of chattel property in permanently indentured servitude

(See Preface, Part I). The State becomes the de facto holder of the Rights to the child (collateral).

Next, the hospital sends the Record of Live Birth to the State Bureau of Vital Statistics, sometimes called the department of Health and Rehabilitative Services (HRS) in some States. Each State is required to supply the Federal government with birth, death, and health statistics. The State agency that receives the Record of Live Birth (title) keeps it and then issues a Birth Certificate (BC). The BC is a commercial instrument (document) evidencing that the State is holding the title (ownership) to the child. Holding the title is not the same as having possession of the property, so the State is the "holder" of the instrument but not the "holder in due course". This is all based on the presumed acceptance of the contract (Record of Live Birth) between the manufacturer (parents) and the purchaser (State). The parents are not aware of this assumed contract because it was never revealed to them nor was full disclosure made in good faith, so they don't object to what they don't know. The current holder of your commercial birth document (receipt) is able to capitalize on it because of your failure to instruct the holder to do otherwise, due to your silence and lack of legal action.

cer·tif·i·cate, noun. Middle English certificat, from Middle French, from Medieval Latin certificatum, from Late Latin, neuter of certificatus, past participle of certificare, to certify, 15th century. 3 : a document evidencing ownership or debt. (Merriam Webster Dictionary 1998). This Birth Certificate issued by the State is then registered with the U.S. Department of Commerce through their agency, the U.S. Census Bureau, who is responsible to collect vital statistics from all the States. The word "registered", in commercial law, does not mean that your name was merely noted in a registry or book for reference purposes. When a Birth Certificate is registered with the U.S. Department of Commerce, it means that the child's persona named on it has become a surety or guarantor as collateral for a commercial loan. registered. Security, bond. (Merriam-Webster's Dictionary of Law 1996). Security. 1a: Something (as a mortgage or collateral) that is provided to make certain the fulfillment of an obligation. Example: used his property as security for a loan. 1b: "surety". 2: Evidence of indebtedness, ownership, or the right to ownership.

Bond. 1a: A usually formal written agreement by which a person undertakes to perform a certain act (as fulfill the obligations of a contract) ...with the condition that failure to perform or abstain will obligate the person ...to pay a sum of money or will result in the forfeiture of money put up by the person or surety. 1b: One who acts as a surety. 2: An interest-bearing document giving evidence of a debt issued by a government body or corporation that is sometimes secured by a lien on property and is often designed to take care of a particular financial need.

Surety. The person who has pledged him or herself to pay back money or perform a certain action if the principal to a contract fails, as collateral, and as part of the original contract. (Duhaime's Law Dictionary).1: a formal engagement (as a pledge) given for the fulfillment of an undertaking. 2: one who promises to answer for the debt or default of another. Under the Uniform Commercial Code, however, a surety includes a guarantor, and the two terms are generally interchangeable. (Merriam-Webster's Dictionary of Law 1996). Guarantor. A person who pledges collateral for the contract of another, but separately, as part of an independently contract with the obligee of the original contract. (Duhaime's Law Dictionary).

It's not difficult to see that a Birth Certificate is a document evidencing debt the moment it's issued. This is how it works: Once each State has registered, by commercial bulk transfer, the Birth Certificates with the U.S. Department of Commerce, the U.S. Department of the Treasury then issues Treasury Securities in the form of Treasury Bonds, Notes, and Bills using the BC's as sureties or guarantors for these purported Securities. This means that the bankrupt corporate U.S. can guarantee to the purchasers of their Securities the lifetime labor of all Americans as collateral for payment. Isn't it nice to know that when you were born, within days you became the collateral for corporate U.S. debt-loans through the assumed contract your parents thought was nothing more than a Record of Live Birth? But wait... the chain of events gets even more interesting.

Who purchases these Treasury Securities? Nearly all are purchased by commercial institutions and brokerage firms on behalf of their individual clients. These purchases are called commercial book entry transactions whereby the individual purchaser never receives a paper stock certificate. Follow very closely and see if you can notice the monopoly and identity of the World Power Brokers unfolding here. Key words are underlined:
1. The commercial book entry system is operated exclusively by the privately owned Federal Reserve System (formerly the Federal Reserve Bank) as fiscal agents of the U.S. Treasury Department
2. All these securities are recorded in the commercial book entry system as "book entry issues" held for the account of the depository institution.
3. The exclusive depository institution is the Depository Trust Company (DTC), a privately owned trust company (bank), who maintains records identifying the individual "beneficial owners" of securities that the DTC holds (holder) in its account in the commercial book entry system.
4. The Depository Trust Company is an operating unit of (owned by) the Federal Reserve System.
5. The Depository Trust Company transfers all the securities to their own private holding company Cede & Company.
6. Cede & Company is the holder of nearly $20 trillion ($ 20,000,000,000,000) of stocks and bonds.
7. The Federal Reserve System uses the Treasury Securities it holds as collateral to print and issue Federal Reserve Notes, which are further debt obligations.
How To Defend Yourself In Court
Chapter 3
In this chapter I will show you how to defend yourself in courts of the United States which are also private corporations set up to adjudicate you under color of law or colorable law. First you have to understand that there are no such thing as judical courts anymore because of the bankruptcy that was filed by President

Roosevelt. There are only administrative courts acting as judicial courts. Supreme Court ruled that there are no Judicial courts in America and there has not been since 1789. Judges do not enforce Statutes and Codes. Executive Administrators enforce Statutes and Codes. (FRC v. GE 281 US 464, Keller v. PE 261 US 428, 1 Stat. 138-178). The Supreme Court is the only court that can rule and have constitutional and original authority over a freeman or a sovereign person. What does that mean? Well anytime that you call yourself a citizen of the United States, you give jurisdiction and authority over the courts to prosecute you because you are using their birth certificate to be under their powers.

A sovereign is someone who has a nationality as a Moor or sovereignty with another nation who has credibility in international law and also has delegation of authority to carry out law. If you have been pulled over by an officer, you must ask him to identify himself. Ask him for his oath of office and delegation of authority from congress because delegation of authority is where authority derives. If he insists on writing you a ticket, you can file an affidavit of fact demanding their oath of office and delegation of authority, and on that same affidavit to the court where you are summoned you challenge jurisdiction of the court because the Supreme Court ruled that "Once jurisdiction is challenged, the court cannot proceed when it clearly appears that the court lacks jurisdiction, the court has no authority to reach merits, but, rather, should dismiss the action." Melo v. US, 505
F2d 1026. [Research Jurisdiction].

In every case there is a plaintiff and there is a defendant. Usually when you are taken to court on behalf of a ticket or other cases you are the defendant. For an example the STATE OF NEW YORK v. JANE DOE. The question you must bring before the court is, "who is the STATE OF NEW YORK and can the STATE OF NEW YORK appear in person because under the 6th amendment you have the right to face your accuser. Of course the STATE OF NEW YORK does not exist but the judge would likely say that the prosecutor is representing the STATE OF NEW YORK. You then turn to the prosecutor and say "for the record can you state your name.After he or she states their name" Then you ask the prosecutor to present identification or a birth certificate with his or her name as the STATE OF NEW YORK. They will not be able to present it. You then say to the prosecutor, "have I committed any crimes against you." They will say no. You then turn to the judge and say, " for the record I would like to demand that this case be dismissed and if not I will be filing a lawsuit against you and the court for fraudulent charges in federal court.

You must remember that in order for a crime to be committed there must be an injured party and the state of NEW YORK can not be injured because it is not a person and it does not exist as a person. Did you know there is no such thing as "Constitutional Rights"? The Constitution does not give you any rights. Your Rights are given to you by God, your Birthright, your Inheritance, Sovereign, and cannot be restricted or taken from you.

Chapter 4
Right To Travel Without Drivers License

What is a drivers license and do you really need one to be able to operate an automobile? The answer is NO. The only people who need a drivers license are those who do business out of their vehicle. For an example, a taxi cab driver or a pizza delivery driver need a license because they operate under commerce. Whenever you are driving and doing business you are operating under commerce therefore whatever you are driving is a commercial vehicle. But if you are traveling from home to work or to visit family then you are not obligated to have a drivers license because you are not doing business out of your automobile. The drivers license can only be required of people who use the highways for trade, commerce or hire; that is, if they earn their living on the road, and they use extraordinary machines on the roads. In other words, if you are not using the highways for profit, you cannot be required to have a drivers license. The Supreme Court ruled in Thompson vs. Smith case, "The right of the citizen to travel upon the public highways and to transport his property thereon, either by carriage or by automobile, is not a mere privilege which a city may prohibit or permit at will, but a common law right which he has under the right to life, liberty, and the pursuit of happiness." Thompson v. Smith, 154 SE 579. There are other cases, just research right to travel.

They say that Identification cards and drivers license identifies who you are, but if these things have an expiration date then it also says that you expire. The question that you should now ask yourself is, do you expire? There was a man by the name of Charlie Sprinkle who brought a lawsuit against Ronald Reagan and his wife and other government officials due to his arrest for not having a drivers

license. Charlie sued Ronald Reagan, Nancy Reagan and numerous other gov-co officials over the driver license, using the foundation that in practice it was a Title of Nobility.
Issuing Titles of Nobility is prohibited by the Constitution and violates the obligation of the subscribed Oath of Office. Ronald Reagan then begged Charlie to drop the lawsuit under the condition that he would make sure that no officer or agent would harras him again. This is because they knew that no citizen needed a drivers license unless they were operating under commerce using their vehicle as a commercial vehicle. Only people who are using their vehicles as a business need a license as all other businesses need a license. So if you are not a taxi cab driver or a bus driver then you DO NOT need a drivers license. (Research Charlie Sprinkle ; Drivers License).

Chapter 5
Bar Association Does Not Qualify You To Practice Law In Court

Lawyers and attorneys are not licensed to practice law. ALL lawyers and judges have membership under the American Bar Association which is a conflict of interest when it comes to being qualified in law. If a judge or a lawyer ever say to you that you have to be licensed and go to law school and pass the bar to be able to practice law, you just tell them that the Supreme Court ruled that ;The practice of Law CAN NOT be licensed by any state/State. (Case: Schware v. Board of Examiners, 353 U.S. 238, 239), or you can say that the practice of Law is AN OCCUPATION OF COMMON RIGHT! (Case: Sims v. Aherns, 271 S.W. 720 (1925).

The American Bar is an offshoot from London Lawyers' Guild and was established by people with invasive monopolistic goals in mind. In 1909 they incorporated this TRAITOROUS group in the state of Illinois and had the State Legislature (which was under the control of lawyers) pass an unconstitutional law that only members of this powerful union of lawyers, called the ABA, could practice law and hold all the key positions in law enforcement and the making of laws. At that time, Illinois became an outlaw state and for all practical purposes, they seceded from the United States of America. The Bar Association then sent organizers to all the other states and explained to the lawyers there how much more profitable and secure it would be for them, as lawyers, to join this union and be protected by its bylaws and cannons. They issued to the lawyers in each state a charter from the Illinois

organization. California joined in 1927 and a few reluctant states and their lawyers waited until the 1930's to join when the treasonous act became DE FACTO and the Citizen's became captives. Under this system, the lawyers could guarantee prejudged decisions for
the privileged class against the lower class.

Chapter 6
Do Not Place Your Trust In Man

Psalms 146:3 / Do not place your trust in man. So what is really going on in this corporation that calls itself the United States? Why are so-called citizens who are children of God being charged for water, electricity, etc, all in which were created by Him who created us. Did God tell man to benefit off of what was rightfully given to us and if not what is the purpose of their intentions? Well this is not complicated to answer, we as man have superior tendencies that is overdone to the point where greed takes over the heart which then creates in man a processed way of thinking. What I mean by a processed way of thinking is that we are born with original or natural minds, but when we allow the flesh to take over the original mind we then start to distribute artificial moral values to our neihbors. Sometimes you can be against something and don't even know that you are supporting that same thing that you are against.

For an example, in the bible it says don't place your faith or trust in man but yet the people that we vote into governmental offices are man. You say, well we need a system to keep everyone under control. Yes I agree, that is true, but why are we just voting these men into office and not questioning their moral values? You vote because satan has conquered and divided two gangs, Democrat and Republicans who work for the same corporation which is the top 10% called the International Bankers I.E. Federal Reserve. The only sovereign powers that America has is war powers because she owes every nation that you see her going up against. Why is America so aggressive when it comes to bringing down nations with the most dominant resources. It is because she is moving all over the earth as it says in the bible spilling the blood of those who are innocent, and the nations who are innocent are the people that she owes. So what does an aggressive gangsta do when he owes someone? They load up and go for the kill.
Jesus was and still is the greatest man to walk the earth, and not one time in his

time here on earth did he show any interest in any government. As a matter of fact it was the government who prosecuted him to be hung on the cross. The government of America has the same policies as the people who crucified Jesus. Do you really think that a Democrat (Pharisees) or a Republican(Saducees) care about your well being more than the One who created you? The United States is expiring because those who are in high places has brought war and assasinated those who came and spoke in the name of God and the reason why they assassinated them is because the truth that Christ said that you shall know came through them little by little and today it is being exposed because God is fed up with the nonsense of not just America but nations who are in bed with her. I'm not saying that man does not have authority, but when the authority you have starts to harm or manipulate those around you then it becomes a problem with God and the Universal energy, and the weapons that America has used and is still making is no match for what God has in store for her.

The Money Changers
Just who are these "Money Changers" James Madison spoke of above?
The Bible tells us that two thousand years ago, Jesus Christ drove the Money Changers from the Temple in Jerusalem, twice. These were the only times Jesus used physical violence. What were Money Changers doing in the Temple?
When Jews came to Jerusalem to pay their Temple tax, they could only pay it with a special coin, the half shekel of the sanctuary. This was a half–ounce of pure silver, about the size of a quarter.

It was the only coin around at that time which was pure silver and of assured weight, without the image of a pagan Emperor. Therefore, to Jews the half–shekel was the coin acceptable to God. But these coins were not plentiful. The Money Changers had cornered the market on them. Then, they raised the price of them – just like any other monopolized commodity – to whatever market would bear.
In other words, the Money Changers were making exorbitant profits because they held a virtual monopoly on money. The Jews had to pay whatever they demanded.

To Jesus injustice violated the sanctity of God's house.
The Money Changers in the Roman Empire
But the money changing scam did not originate in Jesus' day. Two hundred years before Christ, Rome was having trouble with Money Changers.

Two early Roman emperors had tried to diminish the power of the Money Changers by reforming usury laws and limiting land ownership to 500 acres. They both were assassinated. In 48 B.C., Julius Caesar took back the power to coin money from the Money Changers and minted coins for the benefit of all.
With this new, plentiful supply of money, he built great public works projects. By making money plentiful, Caesar won the love common man. But the Money Changers hated him. Some believe this was an important factor in Caesar's assassination.

One thing is for sure, with the death of Caesar came the demise of plentiful money in Rome. Taxes increased, as did corruption. Eventually, the Roman money supply was reduced by 90%. As a result, the common people lost their lands and homes – just as has happened and will happen again in America to the few who still own their own land or homes. With the demise of plentiful money and the loss of their property, the masses lost confidence in Roman government and refused to supportit. Rome plunged into the gloom of the Dark Ages.

Chapter 7
HAARP (High Frequency Active Auroral Research Program)

What I'm about to give to you now may be a bit disturbing to your conscience. What if I told you that the United States has a high powered technology instrument that could control the weather, cause catastrophe's, and even interrupt with the mind of human beings. Well it is true. This instrument is what they call HAARP. It is located in Gakuna, Alaska. It consists of 180 antaenna's with radio waves strong enough to cause earthquakes and these antaenna's are controlled by the U.S. military. HAARP is 3.5 million watts affecting specific concentrated area's of space. HAARP can influence weather anywhere on earth.

The HAARP project
directs a 3.6 MW signal, in the 2.8–10 MHz region of the HF (high-frequency) band, into the ionosphere. The signal may be pulsed or continuous. Then, effects of the transmission and any recovery period can be examined using associated instrumentation, including VHF and UHF radars, HF receivers, and optical cameras. According to the HAARP team, this will advance the study of basic natural processes that occur in the ionosphere under the natural but much stronger influence of solar interaction, and how the natural ionosphere affects

radio signals. If HAARP can create earthquakes and tsunami's then if America is going to invest in this technology it must benefit them in some way. But how? Well if I want an excuse to get into another country
then I must be able to come up with a tactic that will give me a way to help those in a catastrophe that she caused.

The HAARP Induction Magnetometer, a device used to measure the geomagnetic activity induced by the Alaskan HAARP weapon (which has proven to produce earthquakes), began powering up on January 10th at about 4pm UTC lasting on full blast until January 12th at around 3pm UTC, when it powered down again. The Haiti earthquake happened 5-6 hours later. What a coincidence. Did the United States find out that there were some valuable resources in Haiti? Is that why they caused the earthquake to make an excuse to act like they were going over to help the people but in actuality it was an agenda played to conquer land and resources.

What about the Katrina situation? Yes. They blew up a levy using energy from HAARP to pinpoint a certain part of the city that they wanted to depopulate. This shows that man is getting way over their head trying to do what God does, but in the attempt to do so God laugh's. This is how far a nation that says they arte under God would go to obtain the things that will one day be of no use. As the people of God we need to start asking questions and analyzing the things which we think is right and try to find the other persons agenda for what and why they are doing what they are doing.

Former US Secretary of Defense, William Cohen was actually warning us in 1997 that the United States government has developed and is now actively using a weapon that is capable of causing mass destruction by triggering earthquakes, weather modification (inducing heavy rainfall that causes floods or no rainfall which causes droughts), volcanic eruptions and the like. Cohen was warning us about the existence of HAARP. HAARP was developed by the Bill Clinton / Al Gore administration as a United States weapon of mass destruction. HAARP was ordered built by Bill Clinton and Al Gore to beam electromagnetic waves into the Earth's inosphere to trigger geophysical events such as earthquakes, climate modification (change), volcanic eruptions and the like.

Congressional Hearing records during the Clinton administration and HAARP patents disclose that HAARP beaming heats the inosphere. As we all know heat causes things to expand. We also know that heat rises. As HAARP heats one part of the ionosphere the ionosphere expands and gets pushed higher. This HAARP ionosphere heating can cause a controlled diverting or altering of the natural path of jet streams. What does manipulating the jet stream have to do with manipulating the weather? The jet stream is literally a fast flowing (at jet speed) stream – of water vapor. The jet stream transports atmospheric rivers of water vapor around the World.

These jet streams of vapor carry an amount of water vapor roughly equivalent to the average flow of water at the mouth of the Mississippi River. When these atmospheric rivers make landfall, they often release this water vapor in the form of rain or snow. By manipulating the jet stream (pushing or pulling it off course) HAARP can modify the weather. HAARP can alter the path an existing high pressure weather system (clear skies) or low pressure weather system (storm clouds) anywhere on Earth just by heating the ionosphere over the target region. HAARP can also create a column-shaped hole with a diameter of 30 miles that rises a couple of hundred kilometers through the atmosphere. The lower atmosphere then moves up the column to fill in that space, and it changes pressure systems below.

The result of hot surface air being sucked up into the column to fill the HAARP created column-shaped hole is a HAARP created hurricane (if HAARP column shaped hole is made over water) or tornado (if HAARP column-shaped hole is made over land). The April/May 2000 issue of Scientific American contains an article on the effects of altering the course of the jet stream. This slight change to the jet stream path occurred right above the HAARP facility. That little movement created a storm front 4,000 miles away in east Texas and Louisiana to move into central Florida where it triggered a couple of tornadoes.

This article gives evidence that weather modification is certainly possible with only a slight change to the jet stream. In 1998 Bernard Eastlund completed a paperon how to knock out tornadoes using a space-based, solar-collecting microwave generator, which he called theThunderstorm Solar Power Satellite. The microwaves would heat the rainy downdraft inside the storm, disrupting the convective forces needed to concentrate the tornado's power, and so effectively stop it from forming. That paper was presented in Italy and it was so widely accepted that NASA and FEMA contracted Bernard Eastlund to do further research on weather modification using satellite-based technology.

Chapter 8
The Secret Meeting On Jekyll Island

On the Georgian resort hideaway of Jekyll Island, there once met a coalition of Wall Street bankers and U.S. senators. This secret 1910 meeting had a sinister purpose, the conspiracy theorists say. The bankers wanted to establish a new central bank under the direct control of New York's financial elite. Such a plan would give the Wall Street bankers near total control of the financial system and allow them to manipulate it for their personal gain.

In October of 1907 several banking firms, starting with the Knickerbocker Trust Company of New York, collapsed as depositors withdrew funds for fear of unwise investments and misuse of money. Lines of people waited in front of the Knickerbocker to close their accounts. Days later, the Trust Company of America had droves of depositors removing their money. Then, shortly thereafter, a run took place at the Lincoln Trust Company. Across the country apprehension that the panic would continue to spread occurred. In the fall of 1907 the United States was in a recession, it's banking system lacked a lender of last resort mechanism, and an intricate network of directorships, loans, and collateral bonded the fate of many financial institutions together.

Several banking leaders including Jekyll Island Club members George F. Baker, president of the First National Bank, and James Stillman, president of National City Bank, met with financier J. Pierpont Morgan and began examining the assets of the troubled institutions. A decision was made to offer loans to any of the banks that were solvent. The secretary of the treasury George B. Cortelyou was eager to divert the situation and offered the New York bankers use of government funds to help prevent an economic disaster. President Theodore Roosevelt, while the panic of 1907 transpired, was on a hunting trip in Louisiana. Ron Chernow in his book The Death of the Banker offers this account of the 1907 Panic, "In the following days, acting like a one-man Federal Reserve system, [J. Pierpont] Morgan decided which firms would fail and which survive. Through a non stop flurry of meetings, he organized rescues of banks and trust companies, averted a shutdown of the New York Stock Exchange, and engineered a financial bailout of New York City." In the end, the panic was blocked and several young bankers including Henry P. Davison and Benjamin Strong Jr. were recognized for their work organizing personnel and determining the liquidity of the banks involved in the crises. In 1908 J. Pierpont Morgan asked Henry P. Davison to become a partner in his firm J. P. Morgan & Co. and in 1914 Benjamin Strong Jr. was selected to be the first president of the Federal Reserve Bank of New York. Soon after the 1907 panic, Congress formed the National Monetary Commission to review banking policies in the United States. The committee, chaired by Senator Nelson W. Aldrich of Rhode Island, toured Europe and collected data on the various banking methods being incorporated. Using this information as a base, in November of 1910 Senator Aldrich invited several bankers and economic scholars to attend a conference on Jekyll Island. While meeting under the ruse of a duckshooting excursion, the financial experts were in reality hunting for a way to restructure America's banking system and eliminate the possibility of future economic panics.

The 1910 "duck hunt" on Jekyll Island included Senator Nelson Aldrich, his personal secretary Arthur Shelton, former Harvard University professor of economics Dr. A. Piatt Andrew, J.P. Morgan & Co. partner Henry P. Davison, National City Bank president Frank A. Vanderlip and Kuhn, Loeb, and Co. partner Paul M. Warburg. From the start the group proceeded covertly. They began by shunning the use of their last names and met quietly at Aldrich's private railway car in New Jersey. In 1916, B. C. Forbes discussed the Jekyll conference in his book Men Who Are Making America and illuminates, "To this day these financiers are Frank and Harry and Paul [and Piatt] to one another and the late Senator remained 'Nelson' to them until his death. Later [, following the Jekyll conference,]

Benjamin Strong, Jr., was called into frequent consultation and he joined the 'FirstName Club' as 'Ben.'" This book as well as a magazine article by Forbes is the only public mention to the conference until around 1930, when Paul Warburg's book [The Federal Reserve System:] Its Origin and Growth and Nathaniel Wright Stephenson's book Nelson W. Aldrich: A Leader in American Politics were published.

Nathaniel Stephenson, in the Notes section of his biography on Senator Aldrich, suggests that B.C. Forbes learned of the Jekyll conference from an incident taking place at the Brunswick train depot. Stephenson writes, "In the station at Brunswick, Ga., where they ostentatiously talked of sport, the station master gave them a start. 'Gentleman,' said he, 'this is all very pretty, but I must tell you we know who you are and the reporters are waiting outside.' But Mr. Davison was not flustered. 'Come out, old man,' said he, 'I will tell you a story.' They went out together. When Mr. Davison returned he was smiling. 'That's all right,' said he, 'they won't give us away.' The rest is silence. The reporters disappeared and the secret of the strange journey was not divulged. No one asked him how he managed it and he did not volunteer the information." From the Brunswick train station the men boarded a boat and traveled on to Jekyll Island.

The Jekyll Island conference offered a secluded location to discuss banking ideas and enabled the development of a plan that eventually became the Federal Reserve Banking System. The Federal Reserve System is the name given to the twelve central banks regulating America's banking industry and it insures that depositors will not lose their money in the event of funds mismanagement from an accredited bank. Paul Warburg in his book The Federal Reserve System: Its Origin and Growth explains the reason for secrecy behind the meeting. He states, "It is well to remember that the period during which these discussions took place was the time of the struggle of the financial Titans- the period of big combinations of businesses, with bitter fights for control. All over the country there was a deep feeling of fear and suspicion with regard to Wall Street's power and ambitions." Obtaining permission from J. Pierpont Morgan to use the facilities of the Jekyll Island Club, the conference attendees most likely resided in the clubhouse for about ten days. The meeting required long days and late nights of contemplation and reflection. European banking practices were assessed and numerous conversations held regarding the best way to craft a non-partisan banking reform bill. Paul Warburg in the book Henry P. Davison: The Record of a Useful Life recalls, "After we had completed the sketch of the bill, and before setting down to its definitive formulation, it was decided that we had earned 'a day off' which was to be devoted to duck shooting." The Jekyll Island Club was originally formed in 1886 as a hunting preserve and in the 1910s was well stocked with animals such as pheasants and wild hogs. Several ponds on the island attracted numerous game birds and wild ducks.

William Barton McCash and June Hall McCash in the book The Jekyll Island Club: Southern Haven for America's Millionaires offers this narrative of the Jekyll conference. They mention, "How long the surreptitious meeting lasted is uncertain, although the group spent Thanksgiving on the island, where they dined on 'wild turkey with oyster stuffing.' They worked throughout the day and night, taking only sporadic time out to explore Jekyl and enjoy its delights. Aldrich and Davison were both so taken with...[Jekyll Island]... that they joined the club in 1912."

For years members of the Jekyll Island Club would recount the story of the secret meeting and by the 1930s the narrative was considered a club tradition. The conference's solution to America's banking problems called for the creation of a central bank. Although Congress did not pass the reform bill submitted by Senator Aldrich, it did approve a similar proposal in 1913 called the Federal Reserve Act. The Federal Reserve System of today mirrors in essence the plan developed on Jekyll Island in 1910.

The Commission was to study the banking problem and make recommendations to Congress. Of course, the Commission was packed with Morgan's friends and cronies.

The Chairman was a man named Senator Nelson Aldrich from Rhode Island. Aldrich represented the Newport, Rhode Island homes of America's richest banking families and was an investment associate of J.P. Morgan, with extensive bank holdings. His daughter married John D. Rockefeller, Jr., and together they had five sons: John, Nelson (who would become the Vice–President in 1974), Laurence, Winthrop, and David (the head of the Council on Foreign Relations and former Chairman of Chase Manhattan bank).

As soon as the National Monetary Commission was set up, Senator Aldrich immediately embarked on a two–year tour of Europe, where he consulted at length with the private central bankers in England, France and German. The total cost of his trip to the taxpayers was $300,000 – a huge sum in those days. Shortly after his return, on the evening of November 22, 1910, seven of the wealthiest and most powerful men in America boarded Senator Aldrich's private rail car and in the strictest secrecy journeyed to Jekyll Island, off the coast of Georgia.

With Aldrich and three Morgan representatives was Paul Warburg. Warburg had been given a $500,000 per year salary to lobby for passage of a privately-owned central bank in America by the investment firm, Kuhn, Loeb & Company. Warburg's partner in this firm was a man named Jacob Schiff, the grandson of the man who shared the Green Shield house with the Rothschild family in Frankfurt. Schiff, as, we'll later find out, was in the process of spending $20 million to finance the overthrow of the Czar of Russia. These three European banking families, the Rothschilds, the Warburgs, and the Schiffs were interconnected by marriage down through the years, just as were their American banking counterparts, the Morgans, Rockefellers and Aldrich's.

Secrecy was so tight that all seven primary participants were cautioned to use only first names to prevent servants from learning their identities. Years later one participant, Frank Vanderlip, president of Rockefeller's National City Bank of New York and a representative of the Kuhn, Loeb & Company interests, confirmed the Jekyll Island trip in the February 9, 1935 edition of the Saturday Evening Post: "I was as secretive – indeed, as furtive – as any conspirator... Discovery, we knew, simply must not happen, or else all our time and effort would be wasted. If it were to be exposed that our particular group had got together and written a banking bill, that bill would have no chance whatever of passage by Congress."

The participants came together to figure out how to solve their major problem – how to bring back a privately-owned central bank – but there were other problems that needed to be addressed as well. First of all, the market share of the big national banks was shrinking fast.

In the first ten years of the century, the number of U.S. banks had more than doubled to over 20,000. By 1913, only 29% of all banks were National Banks and they held only 57% of all deposits. As Senator Aldrich later admitted in a magazine article:

"Before passage of this Act, the New York bankers could only dominate the reserves of New York. Now, we are able to dominate the bank reserves of the entire county." Therefore, something had to be done to bring these new banks under their control.

As John D. Rockefeller put it: "Competition is a sin." Actually, moralists agree that monopoly abuse is a sin. But why quibble when there's money to be made. Secondly, the nation's economy was so strong that corporations were starting to finance their expansion out of profits instead of taking out huge loans from large banks. In the first 10 years of the new century, 70% of corporate funding came from profits. In other words, American industry was becoming independent of the Money Changers, and that trend had to be stopped.

All the participants knew that these problems could be hammered out into a workable solution, but perhaps their biggest problem was a public relations problem – the name of the new central bank. That discussion took place in one of the many conference rooms in the sprawling hotel now known as the Jekyll Island Club.

Aldrich believed that the word "bank" should not even appear in the name. Warburg wanted to call the legislation the National Reserve Bill or the Federal Reserve Bill. The idea here was to give the impression that the purpose of the new central bank was to stop bank runs, but also to conceal its monopoly character. However, it was Aldrich, the egotistical politician, who insisted it be called the Aldrich Bill.

After nine days at Jekyll Island, the group dispersed. The new central bank (with twelve branches, ultimately) would be very similar to the old Bank of the United States. It would eventually be given a monopoly over the national currency and create that money out of nothing.

How does the Fed "create" money out of nothing? It is a four-step process. But first a word on bonds. Bonds are simply promises to pay – or government IOUs. People buy bonds to get a secure rate of interest. At the end of the term of the bond, the government repays the principal, plus interest (if not paid periodically), and the bond is destroyed. There are about 3.6 trillion dollars worth of these bonds at present. Now here is the Fed moneymaking process:

Step 1. The Fed Open Market Committee approves the purchase of U.S. Bonds on the open market.
Step 2. The bonds are purchased by the New York Fed Bank from whoever is offering them for sale on the open market.
Step 3. The Fed pays for the bonds with electronic credits to the seller's bank, which in turn credits the seller's bank account. These credits are

based on nothing tangible. The Fed just creates them.
Step 4. The banks use these deposits as reserves. They can loan out ten
times the amount of their reserves to new borrowers, all at interest.
In this way, a Fed purchase of, say a million dollars worth of bonds, gets turned
into over 10 million dollars in bank deposits. The Fed, in effect, creates 10% of
this totally new money and the banks create the other 90%.
Actually, due to a number of important exceptions to the 10% reserve ratio, many
loans require no (0%) reserves, making it possible for banks to create many times
more than ten times the money they have in "reserve".
To reduce the amount of money in the economy, the process is just reversed –
the Fed sells bonds to the public, and money flows out of the purchaser's local
bank.

Loans must be reduced by ten times the amount of the sale. So a Fed sale of a
million dollars in bonds, results in 10 million dollars less money in the economy.
So how did the Federal Reform Act of 1913 benefit the bankers whose
representatives huddled at Jekyll Island?
1st – it totally misdirected banking reform efforts from proper
solutions.
2nd – it prevented a proper, debt–free system of government finance –
like Lincoln's Greenbacks – from making a comeback. The bond–based
system of government finance, forced on Lincoln after he created
Greenbacks, was now cast in stone.
3rd – it delegated to the bankers the right to create 90% of our money
supply–based on only fractional reserves – which they could loan out at
interest.
4th – it centralized overall control of our nation's money supply in the
hands of a few men.
5th – it established a new private U.S. central bank with a high degree
of independence from effective political control. Sixteen (16) years after
its creation, the Fed's Great Contraction in the early 1930s would cause
the Great Depression. This independence has been enhanced since then,
through additional amendments.

In order to fool the public into thinking the government retained control, the plan
called for the Fed to be run by a Board of Governors appointed by the President

and approved by the Senate. But all the bankers had to do was to be sure that their
men got appointed to the Board of Governors. That wasn't hard. Bankers have money, and money buys influence over politicians.
Once the participants left Jekyll Island, the public relations blitz was on. The big New York banks pooled a "educational" fund of five million dollars to finance professors at respected universities to endorse the new bank. Woodrow Wilson at Princeton was one of the first to jump on the bandwagon.

But the bankers' subterfuge didn't work. The Aldrich Bill was quickly identified as a bankers bill – a bill to benefit only what had become known as the "Money Trust." As Congressman Lindbergh put it during the Congressional debate:
"The Aldrich Plan is the Wall Street Plan. It means another panic, if necessary, to intimidate the people. Aldrich, paid by the government to represent the people, proposes a plan for the trusts instead."
Seeing they didn't have the votes to win in Congress, the Republican leadership never brought the Aldrich Bill to a vote. President Taft would not back the Aldrich bill. The bankers quietly decided to move to track two, the Democratic alternative. They began financing Woodrow Wilson as the Democratic nominee. He was considered far more tractable than Bryan. As historian James Perloff put it, Wall Street financier Bernard Baruch was put in charge of Wilson's education. To increase Wilson's chances of defeating the popular Taft, they funded the unwitting Teddy Roosevelt in order to split the Republican vote – a tactic often used since to insure getting their man in. The campaigning Roosevelt said:
"Issue of currency should be lodged with the government and be
protected from domination by Wall Street... We are opposed to the
Aldrich Bill because its provisions would place our currency and credit
system in private hands."

This was certainly correct, and it helped draw votes from Taft and got Wilson elected. The National Banking Acts of 1863 & 1864
Prior to the Civil war there were thousands of banks in operation throughout the Union, all of them chartered, that is, licensed by the state governments. Banking regulations were virtually nonexistent. The federal government had no meaningful controls on banking practices, and state regulations were spotty and poorly enforced at best. Economic historians call the era leading up to the Civil

War as the 'state banking era' or the 'free banking era.'

The problems with state banking were numerous, but three were conspicuous. First, the nation had no unified currency. State banks issued their own bank notes as currency, a system which at worst invited severe bouts of counterfeiting and at best introduced additional uncertainty in the task of determining the relative value of each bank note. Second, with no mitigating influence on the issuance of bank notes, the money supply and the price level were highly unstable, introducing and perhaps causing additional volatility in the business cycle. This was due in part to the fact that bank note issuance was frequently tied to the market value of the bank's bond portfolio which they were required to have by law. Third, frequent bank runs resulted in substantial depositor losses and severe crises of confidence in the payments system.

The National Banking Acts of 1863 and 1864 were attempts to assert some degree of federal control over the banking system without the formation of another central bank. The Act had three primary purposes: (1) create a system of national banks, (2) to create a uniform national currency, and (3) to create an active secondary market for Treasury securities to help finance the Civil War (for the Union's side).

The first provision of the Acts was to allow for the incorporation of national banks. These banks were essentially the same as state banks, except national banks received their charter from the federal government and not a state government. This arrangement gave the federal government regulatory jurisdiction over the national banks it created, whereas it asserted no control over state-chartered banks.

National banks had higher capital requirements and higher reserve requirements than their state bank counterparts. To improve liquidity and safety they were restricted from making real estate loans and could not lend to any single person an amount exceeding ten percent of the bank's capital. The National Banking Acts also created under the Treasury Department the office of Comptroller of the Currency. The duties of the office were to inspect the books of the national banks to insure compliance with the above regulations, to hold Treasury securities deposited there by national banks, and, via the Bureau of Engraving, to design and print all national banknotes.

The second goal of the National Banking Acts was to create a uniform national currency. Rather than have several hundred, or several thousand, forms of currency circulating in the states, conducting transactions could be greatly simplified if there were a uniform currency. To achieve this all national banks were required to accept at par the bank notes of other national banks. This insured that national bank notes would not suffer from the same discounting problem with which state bank notes were afflicted. In addition, all national bank notes were printed by the Comptroller of the Currency on behalf of the national banks to guarantee standardization in appearance and quality. This reduced the possibility of counterfeiting, an understandable wartime concern.

The third goal of the Acts was to help finance the Civil War. The volume of notes which a national bank issued was based on the market value of the U.S. Treasury securities the bank held. A national bank was required to keep on deposit with the Comptroller of the Currency a sizable volume of Treasury securities. In exchange the bank received bank notes worth 90 percent, and later 100 percent, of the market value of the deposited bonds. If the bank wished to extend additional loans to generate more profits, then the bank had to increase its holdings of Treasury bonds.

This provision had its roots in the Michigan Act, and it was designed to create a more active secondary market for Treasury bonds and thus lower the cost of borrowing for the federal government.

It was the hope of Secretary of the Treasury Chase that national banks would replace state banks, and that this would create the uniform currency he desired and ease the financing of the Civil War. By 1865 there were 1,500 national banks, about 800 of which had converted from state banking charters. The remainder were new banks. However, this still meant that state bank notes were dominating the currency because most of them were discounted. Accordingly, the public hoarded the national bank notes. To reduced the proliferation of state banking and the notes it generated, Congress imposed a ten percent tax on all outstanding state bank notes. There was no corresponding tax of national bank notes. Many state banks decided to convert to national bank charters because the tax made state banking unprofitable. By 1870 there were 1,638 national banks and only 325 state banks. While the tax eventually eliminated the circulation of state bank notes, it did not entirely kill state banking because state banks began to use checking accounts as a substitute for bank notes. Checking accounts became so popular that by 1890 the Comptroller of the Currency estimated that only ten percent of the nation's money supply was in the form of currency. Combined with lower capital and reserve requirements, as well as the ease with which states issued banking charters, state banks again became the dominant banking form by the late 1880's. Consequently, the improvements to safety that the national banking system offered were mitigated somewhat by the return of state banking. There were two major defects remaining in the banking system in the post Civil War era despite the mild success of the National Banking Acts. The first was the inelastic currency problem. The amount of currency which a national bank could have circulating was based on the market value of the Treasury securities it had deposited with the Comptroller of the Currency, not the par value of the bonds. If prices in the Treasury bond market declined substantially, then the national banks had to reduce the amount of currency they had in circulation. This could be done be refusing new loans or, in a more draconian way, by calling-in loans already outstanding. In either case, the effect on the money supply is a restrictive one. Consequently, the size of the money supply was tied more closely to the performance of the bond market rather than needs of the economy.

Another closely related defect was the liquidity problem. Small rural banks often kept deposits at larger urban banks. The liquidity needs of the rural banks were driven by the liquidity demands of its primary customer, the farmers. In the planting season the was a high demand for currency by farmers so they could make their purchases of farming implements, whereas in harvest season there was an increase in cash deposits as farmers sold their crops. Consequently, the rural banks would take deposits from the urban banks in the spring to meet farmers' withdrawal demands and deposit the additional liquidity in the autumn. Larger urban banks could anticipate this seasonal demand and prepare for it most of the time. However, in 1873, 1884, 1893, and 1907 this reserve pyramid precipitated a financial crisis.

When national banks experienced a drain on their reserves as rural banks made deposit withdrawals, new reserves had to be acquired in accordance with the federal law. A national bank could do this by selling bonds and stocks, by borrowing from a clearinghouse, or by calling-in a few loans. As long as only a few national banks at a time tried to do this, liquidity was easily supplied to the needy banks. However, an attempt en masse to sell bonds or stocks caused a market crash, which in turn forced national banks to call in loans to comply with

Treasury regulations. Many businesses, farmers, or households who had these loans were unable to pay on demand and were forced into bankruptcy. The recessionary vortex became apparent. Frightened by the specter of losing their deposits, in each episode the public stormed any bank rumored, true or not, to be in financial straights. Anyone unable to withdraw their deposits before the bank's till ran dry lost their savings or later received only pennies on the dollar. Private deposit insurance was scant and unreliable. Federal deposit insurance was nonexistent.

The 1907 Banking Panic

The 1907 crisis, also called the Wall Street Panic, was especially severe. The Panic caused what was at that time the worst economic depression in the country's history. It appears to have begun with a stock market crash brought about by a combination of a modest speculative bubble, the liquidity problem, and reserve pyramiding. Centered on New York City, the scale of the crisis reached a proportion so great that banks across the country nearly suspended all withdrawals a kind of self-imposed bank holiday. Several long-standing New York banks fell. The unemployment rate reached 20 percent at the peak of the crisis. Millions lost their deposits as thousands of banks collapsed. The crisis was terminated when J.P. Morgan, a man of sometimes suspicious business tactics and phenomenal wealth, personally made temporary loans to key New York banks and other financial institutions to help them weather the storm. He also made an appeal to the clergy of New York to employ their Sunday sermons to calm the public's fears.

Morgan's emergency injection of liquidity into the banking system undoubtedly prevented an already bad situation from getting still worse. Although private clearinghouses were able to supply adequate temporary liquidity for their members, only a small portion of banks were members of such organizations. What would happen if there were no J.P. Morgan around during the next financial crisis? Just how bad could things really get? There began to emerge both on Wall Street and in Washington a consensus for a kind of institutionalized J.P. Morgan, that is, a public institution that could provide emergency liquidity to the banking system to prevent such panics from starting. The final result of the Panic of 1907 would be the Federal Reserve Act of 1913.

The Federal Reserve Act of 1913

Following the near catastrophic financial disaster of 1907, the movement for banking reform picked up steam among Wall Street bankers, Republicans, and eastern Democrats. However, much of the country was still distrustful of bankers and of banking in general, especially after 1907. After two decades of minority status, Democrats regained control of Congress in 1910 and were able to block several Republican attempts at reform, even though they recognized the need for some kind of currency and banking changes. In 1912 Woodrow Wilson won the Democratic party's nomination for President, and in his populist-friendly acceptance speech he warned against the "money trusts," and advised that "a concentration of the control of credit ... may at any time become infinitely dangerous to free enterprise."

Also in 1910, Senator Nelson Aldrich, Frank Vanderlip of National City (today know as Citibank), Henry Davison of Morgan Bank, and Paul Warburg of the Kuhn, Loeb Investment House met secretly at Jeckyll Island, a resort island off the coast of Georgia, to discuss and formulate banking reform, including plans for a form of central banking. The meeting was held in secret because the participants knew that any plan they generated would be rejected automatically in the House of Representatives if it were associated with Wall Street. Because it was secret and because it involved Wall Street, the Jekyll Island affair has always been a favorite source of conspiracy theories. However, the movement toward significant banking and monetary reform was well-known.[3] It is hardly surprising that given the real possibility of substantial reform, the banking industry would want some sort of input into the nature of the reforms. The Aldrich Plan which the secret meeting produced was even defeated in the House, so even if the Jekyll Island affair was a genuine conspiracy, it clearly failed.

The Aldrich Plan called for a system of fifteen regional central banks, called National Reserve Associations, whose actions would be coordinated by a national board of commercial bankers. The Reserve Association would make emergency loans to member banks, create money to provide an elastic currency that could be exchanged equally for demand deposits, and would act as a fiscal agent for the federal government. Although it was defeated, the Aldrich Plan served as an outline for the bill that eventually was adopted.

The problem with the Aldrich Plan was that the regional banks would be controlled individually and nationally by bankers, a prospect that did not sit well with the populist Democratic party or with Wilson. As the debate began to take shape in the spring of 1913, Congressman Arsene Pujo provided good evidence that the nation's credit markets were under the tight control of a handful of banks the "money trusts" against which Wilson warned.1 Wilson and the Democrats wanted a reform measure which would decentralize control away from the money trusts.

The legislation that eventually emerged was the Federal Reserve Act, also known at the time as the Currency Bill, or the Owen-Glass Act. The bill called for a system of eight to twelve mostly autonomous regional Reserve Banks that would be owned by the banks in their region and whose actions would be coordinated by a Federal Reserve Board appointed by the President. The Board's members originally included the Secretary of the Treasury, the Comptroller of the Currency, and other officials appointed by the President to represent public interests. The proposed Federal Reserve System would therefore be privately owned, but publicly controlled. Wilson signed the bill on December 23, 1913 and the Federal Reserve System was born.

Conspiracy theorists have long viewed the Federal Reserve Act as a means of giving control of the banking system to the money trusts, when in reality the intent and effect was to wrestle control away from them. History clearly demonstrates that in the decades prior to the Federal Reserve Act the decisions of a few large New York banks had, at times, enormous repercussions for banks throughout the country and the economy in general. Following the return to central banking, at least some measure of control was removed from them and placed with the Federal
Reserve.

Chapter 9
Government Controlled Churches

I once asked a scholar in college. Did Jesus need a 501 (c) 3 to be able to preach the word of God. The question stopped there because it was one that could not be answered. Well did he? No. Jesus was a free man and he did not compromise with the government of His time for grants and other things that the government is offering churches today. The now infamous 501(c)(3) section of the Internal Revenue Code (IRC) goes back to 1936.

But then-Senator Lyndon Johnson was the Dr. Frankenstein who, in 1954, unleashed this monster (IRS) upon America. His motivation was that he did not like the way pastors and churches were opposing his liberal agenda, and he wanted to use the power of law to silence them. He, therefore, introduced verbiage to the IRC that churches were prohibited from influencing political legislation and supporting political campaigns, or risk losing their tax-exempt status.

Of course, colonial pastors didn't have to worry about their churches being "incorporated" as State-created (and controlled) entities, or about IRS agents intimidating them regarding what they could or could not say. In early America, preachers were free men; they could say whatever they wanted. Beyond that, virtually everyone regarded preachers as being "God's men," not the "servants of men."

Today, however, the average pastor has become the servant of the State and the church he pastors, more often than not, has become a creature of the State. It is an absolute fact that State-owned churches are killing America.
Dick Greb of the Save-A-Patriot Fellowship in Westminster, Maryland, wrote: "Many Americans find it disturbing that some of our churches today are little more than milquetoast corporations that fear our federal government more than the great

I AM. Moreover, it can even be said that some preachers have the appearance of cringing, 'politically correct' cowards, rather than committed Godly men of fortitude with backbone, such as those we read of in the Bible."
Not only did colonial preachers not have to contend with putting their churches under some State-controlled corporation, they would never have allowed it to happen! Can one imagine Jesus Christ or John The Baptist being told by any State official what he could or could not say, or what his church could or could not do? These men were willing to go to prison or even the grave in order to remain faithful to their spiritual calling and to their political and moral convictions.

The church is supposed to be a force standing alone with the power of God in front of it not the IRS or the government. We as Christians must stand up and demand that the head of the church carry out the orders as Christ did.

Chapter 10
Truth About The Social Security Card

Another way to look at this is: What does "Social Security" really mean? Social means -public. A security is stock of a corporation. Stock is a publicly traded security regulated by the SEC. So when you get a social security number, you are activating or creating the public stock (security) of the corporation known as the United States, stock created for you to use, which adds to their collateral. By getting a social security number you declare yourself to be public stock of the U.S. government. You are a social (public) security, with a security number, you do not get social security insurance. If you will look at the latest issued SS cards, you will see a red number on the back, just like the red registered security numbers on the back of a stock certificate (birth certificate) What's the difference? None. They are both public securities.

If you will remember, the government, in 1894, tried to tax property income with an excise tax, and this lead to the famous Supreme Court case of Pollock v. Farmers' Loan & Trust (1895), that we previously read of. If you remember, the court ruled that property income, real or personal, could only be taxed with a direct tax with apportionment. So the government went back to the drawing boards. The problem? The court had also ruled in other cases, that even corporate property can only be taxed with a direct tax. The solution? The 16th Amendment (1913). It simply stated that all income, from whatever source, such as property, 'connected' to an excise activity, like a corporation, could be taxed with an excise tax. That took care of corporate income. But what about personal income? Another problem?

How can we tax property income with an excise tax? The solution? Create a public corporation for every person in the United States, and have them claim all income received to be connected with that corporation, and thereby subject to an excise tax. But the people would not agree to that if they knew about it, so we must make it look like an old age insurance benefit that they can apply for, since it is

practically impossible for an older person to get life insurance. Result? The Social Security Act of 1935, two years after the U.S. bankruptcy.
By creating social security account, what is really happening is that the government has created a legal fiction (name in all caps), a corporation, for you to use, without your knowledge. Why? Because they can legally tax the property income of a corporation with an excise tax. They cannot tax the sovereign's property income with an excise tax, it can only be done with a direct tax, according to the Constitution. And you voluntarily apply for and use that SS number on everything that you do! It is tied to all income you receive and voluntarily report on tax returns! When you file a tax return, you are declaring that you, the U.S. citizen (corporate property) had income, and corporate property income is taxable with an excise tax.

Chapter 11
Queen Elizabeth And Social Security

Order 1997 Made 22nd of July 1997 coming into force 1st September 1997. At the Court at Buckingham Palace the 22nd day of July 1997. Now, therefore her Majesty in pursuance of section 179 (1) (a) and (2) of the Social Security Administration Act of 1992 and all other powers enabling her on behalf, is pleased, the interest on the loans that were given to the United States. So Alexander Hamilton came up with the great idea of taxing alcohol. The people resisted so George Washington sent out the militia to collect the tax which they did. This has become known as the Whiskey rebellion. It is the Militia's duty to collect taxes. How did the United States collect taxes off of the people if the people are not a party to the Constitution? I'll tell you how. The people are slaves! The United States belongs to the floundering fathers and their posterity and Great Britain. America is nothing more than a Plantation. It always has been. How many times have you seen someone in court inattempt to use the Constitution and then the Judge tells him he can't. It is because you are not a party to it. We are SLAVES!!!!!!! If you don't believe read Padelford, Fay & Co. vs. The Mayor and by and with advise of Her privy Council, to order, and it is hereby ordered as follows:

"This Order may be cited as the Social Security (United States of America) Order 1997 and shall come into force on 1st September 1997."
Does this give a new meaning to Federal Judge William Wayne Justice

stating in court that he takes his orders from England? This order goes on to redefine words in the Social Security Act and makes some changes in United States Law.

Remember, King George was the "Arch-Treasurer and Prince Elector of the Holy Roman Empire and c, and of the United States of America." See: Treaty of Peace (1738) 8 U.S. Statutes at Large. Great Britain which is the agent for the Pope, is in charge of the USA 'plantation.'

What people do not know is that the so called Founding Fathers and King George were working hand-n-hand to bring the people of America to there knees, to install a Central Government over them and to bind them to a debt that could not be paid. First off you have to understand that the UNITED STATES is a corporation and that it existed before the Revolutionary war. See Respublica v. Sweers 1 Dallas 43. 28 U.S.C. 3002 (15)
Now, you also have to realize that King George was not just the King of England, he was also the King of France. Treaty of Peace * U.S. 8 Statutes at Large 80.

On January 22, 1783 Congress ratified a contract for the repayment of 21 loans that the UNITED STATES had already received dating from February 28, 1778 to July 5, 1782. Now the UNITED STATES Inc. owes the King money which is due January 1, 1788 from King George via France. Is this not incredible the King funded both sides of the War. But there was more work that needed to be done. Now the Articles of Confederation which was declared in force March 1, 1781 States in Article 12 " All bills of credit emitted, monies borrowed, and debts contracted by, or under the authority of Congress, before the assembling of the United States, in pursuance of the present confederation, shall be deemed and considered a charge against the United States, for payment and satisfaction whereof the said United States, and the public faith are hereby solemnly pledged."

Now after losing the Revolutionary War, even though the War was nothing more than a move to turn the people into debtors for the King, they were not done yet.

Now the loans were coming due and so a meeting was convened in Annapolis, Maryland, to discuss the economic instability of the country under the Articles of Confederation. Only five States come to the meeting, but there is a call for another meeting to take place in Philadelphia the following year with the express purpose of revising the Articles of Confederation On February 21, 1787 Congress gave approval of the meeting to take place in Philadelphia on May 14, 1787, to revise the Articles of confederation. Something had to be done about the mounting debt. Little did the people know that the so called founding fathers were acutely going to reorganize the United States because it was Bankrupt.

On September 17, 1787 twelve State delegates approve the Constitution. The States have now become Constitutors. Constitutor: In the civil law, one who, by simple agreement, becomes responsible for the payment of another's debt. Blacks Law Dictionary 6th Ed. The States were now liable for the debt owed to the King, but the people of America were not because they were not a party to the Constitution because it was never put to them for a vote On August 4th, 1790 an Act was passed which was Titled: - An Act making provision for the payment of the Debt of the United States. This can be found at 1 U.S. Statutes at Large pages 138-178. This Act for all intents and purposes abolished the States and Created the Districts. If you don't believe it look it up. The Act set up Federal Districts, here in Pennsylvania we got two. In this Act each District was assigned a portion of the debt. The next step was for the states to reorganize their governments which most did in 1790. This had to be done because the States needed to legally bind the people to the debt. The original State Constitutions were never submitted to the people for a vote. So the governments wrote new constitutions and submitted them to people for a vote thereby binding the people to the debts owed to Great Britain. The people became citizens of the State where they resided and ipso facto a citizen of the United States. A citizen is a member of a fictional entity and it is synonymous with subject.

What you think is a state is in reality a corporation, in other words, a Person. "Commonwealth of Pennsylvania is a Person." 9 F. Supp 272 "Word "person" does not include state." 12 Op Atty Gen 176. There are no states, just corporations. Every body politic on this planet is a corporation. A corporation is an artificial entity, a fiction at

law. They only exist in your mind. They are images in your mind, that speak to you. We labor, pledge our property and give our children to a fiction.
Now before we go any further let us examine a few things in the Constitution. Article six section one keeps the loans from the King valid it
states; All Debts contracted and Engagements entered into, before the Adoption of this Constitution, shall be as valid against the United States under this Constitution, as under the Confederation.
Another interesting tidbit can be found at Article One Section
Eight clause Two which states that Congress has the power to borrow money on the credit of the United States. This was needed so the United States (Which went into Bankruptcy on January 1, 1788) could borrow money and then because the States were a party to the Constitution they would also be liable for it.
The next underhanded move was the creation of The United States Bank in 1791. This was a private Bank of which there were 25,000 shares issued of which 18,000 were held by those in England. The Bank loaned the United States money in exchange for Securities of the United States
Now the creditors of the United States which included the King
wanted paid Aldermen of the City of Savannah,

14 Georgia 438, 520 which states: "But, indeed, no private person has a right to complain, by suit in court, on the ground of a breach of the Constitution, the Constitution, it is true, is a compact but he is not a party to it."
Now back to the Militia. Just read Article One Section Eight

Clause (15) which states that it is the militia's job to execute the laws of the Union. Now read Clause (16) Which states that Congress has the power to provide for organizing, arming, and disciplining the Militia, and for governing such part of them as may be employed in the service of the United States .... the Militia is not there to protect you and me, it is there to collect our substance.

As you can plainly see, all the Constitution did is set up a Military Government to guard the King's commerce and make us slaves.
If one goes to 8 U.S. statutes at large 116-132 you will find "The Treaty of Amity, Commerce and Navigation." This Treaty was signed on November 19th, 1794 which was twelve years after the War. Article 2 of

the Treaty states that the King's Troops were still occupying the United States. Being the nice King that he was, he decided that the troops would return to England by June 1st, 1796. The troops were still on American soil because, quite frankly the King wanted them here.

Chapter 12
IRS Is Not Part of The United States Government

The Internal Revenue Service (IRS) is not an agency of the United States government. It is true that not only can it NOT be found in Title 31, but it is nowhere to be found in the entirety of Title 5 U.S.C.

Congress THOUGHT it created it but it didn't. Just look at the 1100 manual and it tells you so. Congress only created the Commissioner's Office. He then hired the private collection agency people and used them as the tax collectors. In fact, I defy you to find any IRS employee listed as an Employee of the United States Government with a United States Employee Identification number that has been hired by any District Director in the country. Now I suggest you look at 27 Code of Federal Regulations Section 250.11 and therein you will find the definition of "Revenue agent." That definition reads "Any duly authorized Commonwealth Internal Revenue Agent of the Department of the Treasury of Puerto Rico." I now refer you to the "Secretary" described in 26 U.S.C. 6301. Does it not state, "The Secretary shall collect the taxes imposed by the internal revenue laws?" Yes it does. Now Congress mandated this by 68A Stat 775 and you cannot disagree. Does not 26 U.S.C. state that this "Secretary" may make a return based on the information he has if a person does not make a return? Yes it does. Does not 26 U.S.C. 6001, 6011 and 6012 refer to this "Secretary?" Yes it does.

Now, if the Revenue agent decides to prosecute, he approaches the Attorney General and this "Secretary" as noted in 26 USC 7401 to prosecute upon concurrence between both the Attorney General and this "Secretary," is this not correct? Yes it is and all the above is undisputable. Is it now contrary to any rational man that this "Secretary" can only be one person and not many. Now, I direct your attention to 27 CFR 250.11 again for the definition of "Secretary" as found in all the above. The defining term for "Secretary" is, "The Secretary of the Treasury of Puerto Rico." That man is Manual Diaz Saldana. Those revenue agents operating in all the states are not United States employees.

The Statute mandated to be at the end of each regulation by 1 Code of Federal Regulations (CFR) is 68A State 775 (26 USC 6301).

I now direct your attention to the House of Representatives, 39th Congress, 2nd Session, Ex. Doc. 99, titled Salary Tax Upon Clerks to Postmasters, LETTER from THE SECRETARY OF THE TREASURY dated Feb. 20, 1867, referred to the House Ways and Means committee and ordered to be printed. I am now going to prove that the IRS agents are not now nor were they ever employees of the United States. You can obtain the document faster than the man on the street. The postmaster wanted to know why postal clerks had to pay income taxes and why the IRS clerks did not have to. The "clerks" are today called "revenue agents." I quote part of the response that is not taken out of context concerning the IRS employees. Why should I, because it is verifiable by anyone.

"No money is advanced by the United States for the payment of such salaries, nor do the assessors perform the duties of disbursing agents of the United States in paying their clerks. The entire amount allowed is paid directly to the assessor, and he is not accountable to the United States for its payment to his clerks, for the reason he has paid them in advance, out of his own funds, and this is reimbursement to him of such amount as the department decides to be reasonable.

No salary tax is therefore collected, or required by the Treasury Department to be accounted for, or paid, on account of payments to assessors' clerks, as the United States pays no such clerks nor has them in its employ or service, and they do not come within the provisions of existing laws imposing such a tax." This was signed by H. McCULLOCH Secretary of the Treasury.

Then to clarify it he included Section 165 which states that the only people to pay income taxes are, and I quote ". . persons in the civil, military, naval, or other employment service of the United States, including senators and representatives and delegates in Congress. "

Since the postal clerks are paid by the United States and the IRS agents were not, those revenue agents were just like me and the millions that do not work or contract with the United States. Therefore they were not subject to the income tax. And so it is today, and that explains why the private collection agency agents

cannot be sued under 26 USC 7214 because they are not employee's of the United States. Today they are based out of and under the direction of the Secretary of the Treasury of Puerto Rico, strictly to collect alcohol, tobacco, and firearms taxable
activities.
The identity of the Secretary is not found in title 26 U.S.C.. The only reference to the identity of the Secretary of the Treasury is in 27 C.F.R. at section 250.11 (definitions) which specifically states: "Secretary means Secretary of the Treasury of Puerto Rico".

Chapter 13
The U.S. Governement /Democracy A Myth

We are not a Democracy. I will repeat this again. We are not a Democratic society. This nation was founded by its creators as a Constitutional Republic. This political theory brought to reality with the birth of our nation guaranteed every man the right to pursue his own happiness. This a generalized definition of freedom. Our forefathers in their great wisdom already knew from experience who could control the people, their money, their quality of life, and even their personal beliefs if a tyrannical government were allowed to. Their experiences with the oppression of the 13 Colonies currency by the King of England's government and the European Bankers was one of the seminal causes of the war for independence. The Real Enemy.

When asking who really controls the US government, let me pose another question. Why do you think President Andrew Jackson abolished the central bank of America? He did this at great peril to himself as European bankers hired assassins to take his life. Answer. Andrew Jackson destroyed the central bank because he knew that the US government would forever be under foreign influence. This, in turn, would control the economy and monetary policy as well as the quality of free markets of this nation when the country's banks were in the hands of foreign interests. Jackson succeeded in ridding America of central banks for 75 years. The United States flourished in that time and expanded its interests internationally by establishing profitable trade with other nations. We did not need a central bank.

How American Citizens Became Enslaved

I've spoken before of the Revenue Act of 1913 and how President Woodrow Wilson brought back the Federal Reserve Bank, income taxes were enacted, and the Revenue Department (IRS) was established. Probably one of the most damaging pieces of law ever brought into existence to plague our nation in its history, the future implications of these acts are immeasurable in view of what followed. In answer to the guarantees of financial stability came the Stock Market Crash of 1929, the Great Depression in the 1930's, inflation, and future recessions from the 1970's on. The supposed advantages of the Federal Reserve have been far outweighed by the liabilities and monetary failures that have transpired of the decades that followed. The Federal Reserve is a cartel of a few private rich families who own and control huge influential banking corporations that have international ties and yet no allegiance to the United States as they are privately. These banks are not owned by the people or the government of the United States. Therefore, they truly have no loyalty to our nation, yet they do profit from America whether that hurts us or not.

The Emergence of TARP
Now, let us ask once again who controls the government of the US? Let me replay recent history for you going back to September 23, 2008. President Bush in response to massive financial market instability and the recent failures of AIG, Bear Sterns, Fannie Mae and Freddie Mac, signed the 700 Billion dollar Troubled Asset Relief Program into existence. The American people were not consulted only told that this act was a necessity. Borne of billions in irresponsible and bad loans made by US Banks, the American taxpayer was elected to ultimately pay for the criminal fiscal mismanagement of the US banking system.

Who Was The Bail Out Really For?
Within 100 days of President Obama's inauguration a 787 Billion dollar bail out was signed into legislation, and the greatest level of government spending since World War II was set into motion during a peace time period. The American Recovery and Investment Act was signed into law February 17, 2009. A multitude of business categories such as the car industry, health insurance, energy, education, and airport screening equipment were targeted for this money. However, many analysts identified much of the bailout payments as going to partisan causes that only came back to the Democrat party by the way of campaign style contributions to leftist causes. Foreign Control Over America Although Senator Ron Paul of Texas had tried to pass legislation to audit the

Federal Reserve for 30 years and once the bill was finally passed shocking revelations came to light. The Federal Reserve had made 16 trillion dollars in secret emergency loans to such recipients as Citigroup, various corporations, foreign banks from France and Scotland, and other US Banks. Loaned to these entities at 0% interest without any repayment as reported by the first audit results by the GAO.

This immense financial activity was conducted beyond the purview of Congress or the knowledge of the people of the United States who would have been out raged had they known about it. The GDP (Gross Domestic Product) of the US is currently 14.12 trillion while the Federal made these unreported loans for 16 trillion, significantly exceeding the total output of the US economy! Remember that Federal Reserve Chairman, Ben Bernanke is appointed, not elected. He also refused to answer Senator Sanders requests for the truth behind an undisclosed 2 trillion dollar loan made months previously.

The Federal Reserve is immensely powerful. As Thomas Jefferson once said, " I believe that banking institutions are more dangerous to our liberties than standing armies. If the American people ever allow private banks to control the issue of their currency, first by inflation, then by deflation, the banks and corporations that will grow up around [the banks] will deprive the people of all property until their children wake-up homeless on the continent their fathers conquered. The issuing power should be taken from the banks and restored to the people, to whom it properly belongs." The Invisible Government That Controls Us Now, do you know who really runs this country? Why we have episodes of recession and inflation, and why we wage war for unfathomable reasons? Look, no further than the Federal Reserve. The Federal Reserve is affiliated with the CFR (Committee on Foreign Relations) which has 4,000 members who range from politicians to media journalists who influence public opinion. Add to these the close association of the Trilateral Commission and you have the major functionaries of the New World Order in the west. These organizations primarily encompass a global, one world government that is a collectivist entity, dedicated to the subjugation of the human population through trans-generational continued worldwide leadership.

These elitists think they have the right to rob our freedoms and manipulate our lives through a myriad of political and social schemes. This is the enemy. It is not a conspiracy. It is not a shot in the dark aimed at a frivolous target of mine or anyone else's misdirected anger. This is the truth as dismaying as it may seem. As the old saying goes, " if you want a cure, know the cause." I have informed you of the cause.

The Problem
There was a time in this country when to ask someone for whom he worked was considered somewhat insulting, as it implied he was an incompetent, incapable of gainful self–employment. But now, property ownership (net wealth) is not a general feature of our society, as it was before the Civil War, and largely was still until the Great Depression.

Rather, net debt and complete dependence on a precarious wage or salary at the will of others is the general condition. Since the exercise of freedom often includes using material objects such as books, food, clothing, shelter, arms, transport, etc., the choice and possession of which requires some wealth, we are forced to admit that the general condition of Americans is one of increasing dependence and limitations on our freedom.

Since the turn of the century, there has occurred throughout the world a major increase in debt and a major decline in the freedom of individuals, and of states, toconduct their own affairs. To restore a condition of widespread, modest wealth is therefore essential to regaining and preserving our freedom.
What's going on in America today? Why are we over our heads in debt? Why can't the politicians bring debt under control? Why are so many people – often both parents now – working at low–paying, dead–end jobs and still making do with less? What's the future of the American economy and way of life?
Why does the government tell us inflation is low, when the buying power of our paychecks is declining at an alarming rate? Only a generation ago, bread was a quarter and you could get a new car for $1,995!
Are we headed into an economic crash of unprecedented proportions – one which will make the crash of 1929 and the Great Depression which followed look like a Sunday school picnic? If so, can we prevent it? Or, will we simply arrive at the same point through more inflation–caused poverty, robbing Americans of their savings, fixed incomes and wages by imperceptible degrees – reducing their purchasing power. What can we do to protect our families?

Some reliable experts say a crash is coming. They also say that there are simple, inexpensive things anyone can do to protect their families – to keep food on the table and a roof over our heads even in the worst of times. But to do that, we have to understand why a depression is coming, who's behind it, what they want, and how the perpetrators plan on protecting their families. Armed with this knowledge, any of us can ride out the coming storm.

Larry Bates was a bank president for eleven years. As a member of the Tennessee House of Representatives, he chaired the committee on Banking and Commerce. He's also a former professor of economics and the author of the best–selling book, The New Economic Disorder.

I can tell you right now that there is going to be a crash of unprecedented proportions. A crash like we have never seen before in this country. The greatest shock of this decade is that more people are about to loose more money then at any time before in history, but the second greatest shock will be the incredible amount of money a relatively small group of people will make at the same time. You see, in periods of economic upheaval, in periods of economic crisis, wealth is not destroyed, it is merely transferred." – Larry Bates
Banker and former Presidential candidate Charles Collins is a lawyer, has owned banks, and served as a bank director. He believes we'll never get out of debt because the Federal Reserve is in control of our money.
"Right now, it's perpetuated by the Federal Reserve making us borrow the money from them, at interest, to pay the interest that's already accumulated. So we cannot get out of debt the way we're going now."
Economist Henry Pasquet is a tenured instructor in economics. He agrees the end is near for the U. S. economy. "No, not when you are adding roughly a billion dollars a day. We just can't go on.

We had less than 1 trillion dollars of national debt in 1980, now it's $5 trillion – 5 times greater in 15 years. It just doesn't take a genius to realize that this just can't go on forever." The problem is we have one of the worst monetary systems ever devised – a central bank that operates independently of our government, which, with other private banks, creates all of our money with a parallel amount of interest–bearing debt. That's why we can never get out of debt. And that's why a deep depression is a certainty, for most of our citizens, whether caused suddenly in a severe economic crash, or gradually through continued relentless inflation.

The Fed is creating it to enrich its private stockholders, just like it deliberately created the Great Depression the 1930s.

The Federal Reserve headquarters is in Washington, D.C. It sits on a very impressive address right on Constitution Avenue, right across from the Lincoln Memorial. But is it "Federal"? Is it really part of the United States government? Well, what we are about to show you is that there is nothing federal about the Fed Reserve, and there are no reserves. The name is a deception created back before the Fed Reserve Act was passed in 1913 to make Americans think that America's new central bank operates in the public interest.
The truth is that the Fed is a private (or best, quasi–public) bank, owned by private National banks which are the stockholders, and run for their private profit. "That's exactly correct; the Fed is privately–owned, for–profit corporation which has no reserves, at least no reserve to back up the Federal Reserve notes which are our common currency." – Economist Henry Pasquet.

The Federal Reserve Act was railroaded through a carefully prepared Congressional Conference Committee scheduled during unlikely hours of 1:30 a.m. to 4:30 a Monday, December 22, 1913, when most members were sleeping, at which 20–40 substantial differences in the House and Senate versions were supposedly described, deliberated, debated, reconciled and voted upon in a near miraculous 4 1/2 to 9 minutes per item, at that late hour. As author Anthony C. Sutton noted:
"This miracle of speediness, never equaled before or after in the U.S. Congress, is ominously comparable to the rubber stamp lawmaking of the banana republics."
At 4:30 a.m. a prepared report of this Committee was handed to the printers. Senator Bristow of Kansas, the Republican leader, stated on the Congressional Record that the Conference Committee had met without notifying them and that Republicans were not present, and was given no opportunity to either read or sign the Conference Committee report.
The Conference report is normally read on the Senate floor. The Republicans did not even see the report. Some Senators stated on the floor of the Senate that they had no knowledge of the contents of the Bill. At 6:02 p.m., December 23rd, when many members had already left the Capitol for the Christmas holiday, the very same day the Bill was hurried through the House and Senate, President Woodrow Wilson signed the Federal Reserve Act of l913 into law.
The Act transferred control of the money supply of the United States from

Congress to a private banking elite. It is not surprising that a bill granting a few national bankers a private money monopoly was passed in such a corrupted manner. As author Anthony C. Sutton noted:
"The Federal Reserve System is a legal private monopoly of the money supply operated for the benefit of the few under the guise of protecting and promoting the public intent." Heroic Nebraska Senator Hitchcock, the only Senate Democrat working against the bill, had proposed numerous amendments to the bill aimed at making the Federal Reserve System a government agency (i.e. placing control in the Department of the Treasury), rather than a private monopoly, but these were all tabled – so great was
the power of the Money Changers over Congress by then.
If there's still any doubt whether the Federal Reserve is a part of the U.S. government, check your local telephone book. It's not listed in the blue "government pages." It is correctly listed in the "business" white pages, right next to Federal Express, another private company. But more directly, U.S. Courts have ruled that the Fed is a special form of a Private Corporation.
Let's take a look at the Fed shareholders: according to researcher Eric Samuelson, as of November, 1997, the Federal Reserve Bank of New York (which completely dominates the other eleven branches through stock ownership, control, influence, having the only permanent voting seat on the Federal Open Market Committee and by handling all open market bond transactions), which has 19,752,655 shares outstanding, was majority–owned by two banks – Chase Manhattan bank (now merged with Chemical Bank) with 6,389,445 shares or 32.35%, and Citibank, N.A., with 4,051,851 shares or 20.51%. Together those two banks own 10,441,295 shares or 52.86%: majority control.
While majority ownership conclusively demonstrates effective control, it is not critical to control, which is often exercised in large, publicly–traded corporations by blocks of as little as 25%, and even 2%, when the other owners hold smaller blocks. Why can't Congress do something about this dangerous concentration of power. Most members of Congress just don't understand the system, and the few who do are afraid to speak up. For example, initially a veteran Congressman asked us if he could be interviewed. However, both times our camera crew arrived at his office to do the interview, we were not able to film. The Congressman never appeared, and eventually got cold feet and withdrew.
Fighting the bankers is a good way to see one's opponent get heavily funded in the next election. But a few others in Congress have been bolder over the years. Here are three quick examples.

In 1923, Representative Charles A. Lindbergh, a Republican from Minnesota, the father of famed aviator, "Lucky" Lindy, put it this way,
The financial system has been turned over to the Federal Reserve Board. That board administers the finance system by authority of ... a purely profiteering group. The system is private, conducted for the sole purpose of obtaining the greatest possible profits from the use of other people's money."

One of the most outspoken critics in Congress of the Fed was the Chairman of the House Banking and Currency Committee during the Great Depression years, Louis T. McFadden (R–PA). He said in 1932:
"We have in this country one of the most corrupt institutions the world has ever known. I refer to the Federal Reserve Board ... This evil institution has impoverished ... the people of the United States ... and has practically bankrupted our Government. It has done this through ... the corrupt practices of the moneyed vultures who control it."

Senator Barry Goldwater was a frequent critic of the Fed:
"Most Americans have no real understanding of the operation of the international moneylenders ... The accounts of the Federal Reserve System have never been audited. It operates outside the control of Congress and ... manipulates the credit of the United States" Does that power affect you? "The Fed really is more powerful than the federal government. It is more powerful
than the President, Congress or the courts. Let me prove my case. The Fed determines what the average person's car payment and house payment is going to be and whether they have a job or not. And I submit to you – that is total control. The Fed is the largest single creditor of the U.S. government. What does Proverbs tell us? The borrower is servant to the lender." – Larry Bates
What one has to understand is that from the day the Constitution was adopted right up to today, the folks who profit from privately owned central banks, like the Fed, or, as President Madison called them, the "Money Changers", have fought a running battle for control over who gets to issue America's money.
Why is who issues the money so important? Think of money as just another commodity. If you have a monopoly on a commodity that everyone needs, everyone wants, and nobody has enough of, there are lots of ways to make a profit and also exert tremendous political influence.

That's what this battle is all about. Throughout the history of the United States, the money power has gone back and forth between Congress and some sort of privately-owned central bank. The American people fought off four privately-owned central banks, before succumbing to the first stage of a fifth privately-owned central bank during a time of national weakness – the Civil War.
The founding fathers knew the evils of a privately-owned central bank. First of all, they had seen how the privately-owned British central bank, the Bank of England, had run up the British national debt to such an extent that Parliament had been forced to place unfair taxes on the American colonies.

In fact, as we'll see later, Ben Franklin claimed that this was the real cause of the American Revolution. Most of the founding fathers realized the potential dangers of banking, and feared bankers' accumulation of wealth and power. Jefferson put it this way:

"I sincerely believe that banking institutions are more dangerous to our liberties than standing armies. Already they have raised up a money aristocracy that has set the government at defiance. The issuing power should be taken from the banks and restored to the people to whom it properly belongs."
That succinct statement of Jefferson is in fact, the solution to most of our economic problems today. James Madison, the main author of the Constitution, agreed.

Interestingly, he called those behind the central bank scheme "Money Changers." Madison strongly criticized their actions:
"History records that the Money Changers have used every form of abuse, intrigue, deceit, and violent means possible to maintain their control over governments by controlling money and its issuance."
The battle over who gets to issue our money has been the pivotal issue through the history of the United States. Wars are fought over it. Depressions are caused to acquire it. Yet after World War I, this battle was rarely mentioned in newspapers or history books. Why?

Media Control and the International Bankers
By World War I, the Money Changers, with their dominant wealth, had seized control of most of the nation's press. In a 1912 Senate Privileges and Elections Committee hearing, a letter was introduced to the Committee written by

Representative Joseph Sibley (PA), a Rockefeller agent in Congress, to John D. Archibald, a Standard Oil employee of Rockefeller's, which read in part: "An efficient literary bureau is needed, not for a day or a crisis but a permanent healthy control of the Associated Press and kindred avenues. It will cost money but will be cheapest in the end."

John Swinton, the former Chief of Staff of the New York Times, called by his peers "the Dean of his profession", was asked in 1953 to give a toast before the New York Press Club. He responded with the following statement:
"There is no such thing as an independent press in America, if we except that of little country towns. You know this and I know it. Not a man among you dares to utter his honest opinion. Were you to utter it, you know beforehand that it would never appear in print.
I am paid one hundred and fifty dollars a week so that I may keep my honest opinion out of the newspaper for which I write. You too are paid similar salaries for similar services. Were I to permit that a single edition of my newspaper contained an honest opinion, my occupation – like Othello's – would be gone in less than twenty-four hours.
The man who would be so foolish as to write his honest opinion would soon be on the streets in search of another job. It is the duty of a New York journalist to lie, to distort, to revile, to toady at the feet of Mammon, and to sell his country and his race for his daily bread, or what amounts to the same thing, his salary.

We are the tools and the vassals of the rich behind the scenes. We are marionettes. These men pull the strings and we dance. Our time, our talents, our lives, our capacities are all the property of these men – we are intellectual prostitutes." (As quoted by T. St. John Gaffney in Breaking The Silence, page 4.)

That was the U.S. press in 1953. It is the mass media of America today. Press control, and later electronic media control (radio and TV), was seized in carefully planned steps, yielding the present situation in which all major mass media and the critically important major reporting services, which are the source of most news and upon which most news is based, are controlled by the Money Changers. Representative Callaway discussed some of this press control in the Congressional Record, Vol. 54, Feb. 9, 1917, p. 2947:

"In March, 1915, the J.P. Morgan interests, the steel, shipbuilding, and powder interests, and their subsidiary organizations, got together 12 men high up in the newspaper world and employed them to select the most influential newspapers in the United States and sufficient number of them to control generally the policy of the daily press.

They found it was only necessary to purchase the control of 25 of the greatest papers.. An agreement was reached; the policy of the papers was bought, to be paid for by the month; an editor was furnished for each paper to properly supervise and edit information regarding the questions of preparedness, militarism, financial policies, and other things of national and international nature considered vital to the interests of the purchasers."
"So far as can be learned, the Rockefellers have given up their old policy of owning newspapers and magazines outright, relying now upon the publications of all camps to serve their best interests in return for the vast volume of petroleum and allied advertising under Rockefeller control. After the J.P. Morgan bloc, the Rockefellers have the most advertising of any group to dispose of. And when advertising alone is not sufficient to insure the fealty of a newspaper, the Rockefeller companies have been known to make direct payments in return for a friendly editorial attitude."
A few years ago, three-quarters of the majority stockholders of ABC, CBS, NBC and CNN were banks, such as Chase Manhattan Corp., Citibank, Morgan Guaranty Trust and Bank of America; ten such corporations controlled 59 magazines (including Time and Newsweek), 58 newspapers (including the New York Times, the Washington Post, the Wall Street Journal), and various motion picture companies, giving the major Wall Street banks virtually total ownership of the mass media, with few exceptions (such as the Disney Company's purchase of ABC).

Only 50 cities in America now have more than one daily paper, and they are often owned by the same group. Only about 25% of the nation's 1,500 daily papers are independently owned. This concentration has been rapidly accelerating in recent years and ownership is nearly monolithic now, reflecting the identical control described above. Of course, much care is taken to fool the public with the appearance of competition by maintaining different corporate logos, anchorpersons and other trivia, projecting a sense of objectivity that belies the uniform underlying bank ownership and editorial control. This accounts for the total blackout on news coverage and investigative reporting of banker control of our country.

Nevertheless, throughout U.S. history, the battle over who gets the power to issue our money has raged. In fact it has changed hands back and forth eight times since 1694, in five transition periods which may aptly be described as "Bank Wars" (or more precisely: Private Central Bank vs. American People Wars), yet this fact has virtually vanished from public view for over three generations behind a smoke screen emitted by Fed cheerleaders in the media.

Chapter 14
Rise of The Rothschilds / Illuminati

This is Frankfurt, Germany. Fifty years after the Bank of England opened its doors, a goldsmith named Amschel Moses Bauer opened a coin shop – a counting house in 1743, and over the door he placed sign depicting a Roman eagle on a red shield. The shop became known as the Red Shield firm, or in German Rothschild. When his son, Meyer Amschel Bauer, inherited the business, he decided to change name to Rothschild.

Meyer Rothschild soon learned that loan money to governments and kings was more profitable than loaning to private individuals. Not only were the loans bigger, but they were secured by the nation's taxes.

Meyer Rothschild had five sons. He trained them all in the secret techniques of money creation and manipulation, then sent them to the major capitals of Europe to open branch offices of the family banking business. It is directed that one son in each generation was to rule the family business; women were excluded.
His first son, Amschel, stayed in Frankfurt to mind the hometown bank. His second son, Salomon was sent to Vienna. His third son, Nathan was clearly the most clever. He was sent to London at age 21, in 1798, a hundred years after the founding of the Bank of England. His fourth son, Karl, went to Naples. His fifth son, Jakob (James), went to Paris.

There is evidence that when the five brothers spread out to the five provinces of the financial empire of Europe, they had some secret help for the accumulation of these enormous sums ... that they were the treasurers of

this first Comintern .. But others say, and I think with better reason, that the Rothschilds were not the treasurers, but the chiefs ..." – C.G. Rakovsky
In 1785, Meyer moved his entire family to a larger house, a five story dwelling he shared with the Schiff family. This house was known the "Green Shield" house. The Rothschilds and the Schiffs would play a central role in the rest of European financial history, and in that the United States and the world. The Schiffs' grandson moved to New York and helped fund the Bolshevik coup d'état in 1917 in Russia.

The Rothschilds broke into dealings with European royalty in Wilhelmshohe, the palace of the wealthiest man in Germany – in fact, the wealthiest monarch in all of Europe – Prince William of Hesse–Cassel.

At first, the Rothschilds were only helping William speculate in precious coins. But when Napoleon chased Prince William into exile, William sent £550,000 (a gigantic sum at that time, equivalent to many millions of current U.S. dollars) to Nathan Rothschild in London with instructions from him to buy Consola – British government bonds also called government stock. But Rothschild used the money for his own purposes. With Napoleon on the loose, the opportunities for highly profitable wartime investments were nearly limitless.

William returned to Wilhelmshohe, sometime prior to the Battle of Waterloo in 1815. He summoned the Rothschilds and demanded his money back.
The Rothschilds returned William's money, with the 8% interest the British Consols would have paid him had the investment actually been made. But the Rothschilds kept all the vast wartime profits they had made using Wilhelm's money–shady practice in any century.

Partly by such practices, Nathan Rothschild was able to later brag that in the seventeen years he had been in England, he had increased his original £20,000 stake given to him by his father by 2,500 times (=£50,000,000), a truly vast sum at that time, comparable to billions of current U.S. dollars in purchasing power.
As early as 1817, the director of the Prussian Treasury, on a visit to London, wrote that Nathan Rothschild had incredible influence upon all financial affairs here in London.

It is widely stated ... that he entirely regulates the rate of exchange in the City. His power as a banker is enormous."
Austrian Prince Metternich's secretary wrote of the Rothschilds as early as 1818
That they are the richest people in Europe.
By cooperating within the family, using fractional reserve banking techniques, the Rothschilds' banks soon grew unbelievably wealthy. By the mid–1800s, they dominated all European banking, and were certainly the wealthiest family in the world. A large part of the profligate nobility of Europe became deeply indebted to them. In virtue of their presence in five nations as bankers, they were effectively autonomous – an entity independent from the nations in which they operated. If one nation's policies were displeasing to them or their interests, they could simply do no further lending there, or lend to those nations or groups opposed to such policies. Only they knew where their gold and other reserves were located, thus shielding them from government seizure, penalty, pressure or taxation, as well as effectively making any national investigation or audit meaningless. Only they knew the extent (or paucity) of their fractional reserves, scattered in five nations a tremendous advantage over purely national banks engaging in fractional reserve banking too.

It was precisely their international character that gave them unique advantages over national banks and governments, and that was precisely what rulers and national parliaments should have prohibited, but did not. This remains true of international or multinational banks to this very day, and is the driving force of globalization – the push for one–world government.

The Rothschilds provided huge loans to establish monopolies in various industries, thereby guaranteeing the borrowers' ability to repay the loans by raising prices without fear of price competition, while increasing the Rothschild's economic and political power.

They financed Cecil Rhodes, making it possible for him to establish a monopoly over the gold fields of South Africa and the de Beers over diamonds. In America, they financed the monopolization of railroads. The National City Bank of Cleveland, which was identified in Congressional hearings as one of three Rothschild banks in the United States, provided John D.
Rockefeller with the money to begin his monopolization of the oil refinery

business, resulting in Standard Oil. Jacob Schiff, who had been born in the Rothschild "Green Shield" house in Frankfurt and who was then the principal Rothschild agent in the U.S., advised Rockefeller and developed the infamous rebate deal Rockefeller secretly demanded
from railroads shipping competitors' oil.
These same railroads were already monopolized by Rothschild control through agents and allies J.P. Morgan and Kuhn, Loeb & Company (Schiff was on the Board) which together controlled 95% of all U.S. railroad mileage.
By 1850, James Rothschild, the heir of the French branch of the family, was said to be worth 600 million French francs – 150 million more than all the other bankers in France put together.

James had been established in Paris in 1812 with a capital of $200,000 by Mayer Amschel. At the time of his death in 1868, 56 years later, his annual income was $40,000,000. No fortune in America at that time equaled even one year's income of James. Referring to James Rothschild, the poet Heinrich Heine said:
"Money is the god of our times, and Rothschild is his prophet."
James built his fabulous mansion, called Femeres, 19 miles northeast of Paris. Wilhelm I, on first seeing it exclaimed, "Kings couldn't afford this. It could only belong to a Rothschild." Another 19th century French commentator put it this way:
"There is but one power in Europe and that is Rothschild."
There is no evidence that their predominant standing in European or world finance has changed, to the contrary, as their wealth has increased they have simply increased their "passion for anonymity". Their vast holdings rarely bear their name.

Author Frederic Morton wrote of them that they had "conquered the world more thoroughly, more cunningly, and much more lastingly than all the Caesars before..."

Now let's take a look at the results the Bank of England produced on the British economy, and how that later was the root cause of the American Revolution. Now it was time for the Money Changers to get back a new, private central bank for America, the fifth private central bank to control and manipulate America's money supply.

A major final panic would be necessary to focus the nation's attention on the supposed need for a central bank. The thin rationale offered was that only a central bank can prevent widespread bank failures and stabilize the currency. The critically important feature of who would own and control it was an issue carefully avoided.

Before the Civil War, the Rothschilds had previously used, as principal agents in the U.S., J.L and S.I Joseph & Company. Later, George Peabody, an American bond salesman, traveled to London before the Civil War and developed a relationship with Nathan Rothschild, which became a highly profitable one for Peabody. His business expanding, he took on an American partner, Junius Morgan, father of J.P. Morgan.

In 1857 Junius was the recipient of a £800,000 loan from the Bank of England at a time of financial crisis when many other firms were denied such loans. Junius Morgan became the Union's financial agent in Britain, often closely associated with the Rothschilds.

In the post–Civil War period the connection between Morgan and the Rothschilds was certainly well known in financial circles. As one writer noted:
"Morgan's activities in 1895–1896 in selling U.S. gold bonds in Europe
were based on his alliance with the House of Rothschild."
After his father's death, J.P. Morgan took on a British partner, Edward Grenfell, a long–time director of the Bank of England. There is speculation the Morgans became the Rothschilds' principal agents in the U.S., eventually to be eclipsed by the Rockefellers.

Early in this century, in U.S. finance, the press and in politics, all lines of power converged on the financial houses of J.P. Morgan (J.P. Morgan Company; Bankers Trust Company; First National Bank of New York, Guaranty Trust), the Rockefellers (National City Bank of New York; Chase National Bank; Chemical Bank); Kuhn, Loeb & Company (a representative of the Rothschild banks; National City Bank of New York) and the Warburg's (Manhattan Corp. bank). Morgan was clearly the most powerful banker in America, and like his father, worked as an agent for the Rothschild family, but also for his own interests. He helped finance the monopolization of various industries, consolidated big steel holdings into a monopoly by buying Andrew Carnegie's steel companies, and owned numerous industrial companies and banks.

Interestingly, though reputedly America's richest banker, upon J.P.'s death, his estate contained $68 million dollars, only 19% of J.P. Morgan company. The bulk of the securities most people thought he owned, were in fact owned by others. When J.P. Morgan, Jr. (Jack) died in 1943, his estate was valued at only $16 million. By contrast, when Alphonse Rothschild died in 1905 his estate contained $60 million in U.S. securities alone.

John D. Rockefeller and his brother William used their enormous profits from the Standard Oil monopoly to dominate the National City Bank, merged in 1955 with Morgan's and Kuhn, Loeb & Company's First National Bank of New York, which resulted in Citibank (Citicorp).

Similarly, John D. bought control of Chase National Bank, and merged it with Warburg's Manhattan bank, resulting in the Rockefeller–dominated Chase Manhattan bank, recently merged with the Rockefeller–controlled Chemical Bank. The combination of the Rockefeller–controlled Chase–Manhattan/Citicorp banks gives them majority control over the New York Fed (52%), which completely dominates the Federal Reserve System. But the New York Fed was controlled by Rockefeller long before any majority ownership was reached.
By these mergers, the Rockefellers gradually replaced the Morgans, Schiffs and Warburgs as the principal Rothschild allies in the U.S.
Recent 1998 mega–bank mergers have further consolidated this monolithic control.

David Rockefeller, retired Chairman, was the point man for the Rockefellers in recent decades. One wag described the Rockefellers' seventy–five palatial Pocantico Hills residences (on over 4,000 acres) in New York as "the kind of place God would have built if he had had the money."
In Europe a similar consolidation resulted in two main banking dynasties – the Warburgs and the Rothschilds. But whereas the Morgans and the Rockefellers were relatively fierce competitors until the famous Northern Securities battle resulted in a sort of truce, the Warburgs have always been subordinate to the Rothschilds and have not seriously challenged them.

The relationship between the Rothschilds and Rockefellers was initially one of debtor/creditor, as the Rothschilds provided the seed money for J.D. Rockefeller to monopolize the U.S. oil refinery business and most oil pipelines. Subsequently, the relationship entered into measured competition here (local wars between subordinates sometimes resulting) and cooperation there, but like the competition between the other banks, this too has resolved into a power sharing arrangement.

The centers of power are not easy to identify and remain to a large extent hidden through carefully concealed and interlocking directorships, off-shore accounts, nominee holdings, private foundations, trusts and the rest. But the top international bankers are vested with the last word in economic and political power.

Most commentators are of the opinion that the Rothschilds are definitely the dominant partner; citing for example, the 1950's appointment of J. Richardson Dilworth, partner of Kuhn, Loeb & Co. (a satellite of the Rothschild family) who left to take control of the Rockefeller family purse strings, where he managed the investments of Rockefeller descendants in as many as 200 private foundations. However, the operative relationship described by Georgetown historian Carroll Quigley is "feudalistic", that is, analogous to the relationships between a feudal king and the aristocracy consisting of dukes, earls, barons, etc., all mutually supportive, while safeguarding their own turf and "independence", expanding it when permitted without violating the fundamental hierarchical relationships – violations can result in wars.

Lesser members of this "feudalistic" international banking plutocracy include or have included, the Sassoons (in India and the Far East); Lazard Freres France; Mendelsohn (Netherlands); Israel Moses Seif (Italy); Kuhn, Loeb (U.S.); Goldman Sachs (U.S.) Lehman Bros. (U.S.); Schroeders (Germany); Hambros (Scandinavia), the Bethmanns, Ladenburgs, Erlangers, Sterns, Seligmans, Schiffs, Speyers, Abs, Mirabauds, Mallets, Faulds, and many others.
The ruling clique in most nations now, excepting a portion of the Muslim world and a few so called "rogue" states, are equivalent to local barons, subservient to the higher banking dukes, earls, etc.

This generally reaches right down to the city level, where the dominant local bankers are usually the petty aristocracy, affiliated through banking and

commercial relationships with their banking "barons" and so on.
As Georgetown historian Professor Carroll Quigley has noted, if it were possible to detail the asset portfolios of the banking plutocrats one would find the title-deeds of practically all the buildings, industries, farms, transport systems and mineral resources of the world. Accounting for this, Quigley wrote:
"Their secret is that they have annexed from governments, monarchies, and republics the power to create the world 's money on debt–terms requiring tribute both in principal and interest."

Unfortunately, rather than benevolent rulers, this international banking plutocracy has taken the Malthusian position that the world is overpopulated with serfs, and, at the highest levels, they are deadly serious about correcting this "threat" and "imbalance", whatever the cost in human misery and suffering.
To return to 1902: President Theodore Roosevelt allegedly went after Morgan and his friends by using the Sherman Anti–Trust Act to try to break up their industrial monopolies. Actually, Roosevelt did very little to interfere in the growing monopolization of American industry by the bankers and their surrogates.
For example, Roosevelt supposedly broke up the Standard Oil monopoly. But it wasn't really broken up at all. It was merely divided into seven corporations, all still controlled by the Rockefellers, who had been originally financed by the Rothschild–controlled National City Bank of Cleveland. The public was aware of this thanks to political cartoonists like Thomas Nast who referred to the bankers as the "Money Trust."

By 1907, the year after Teddy Roosevelt's re–election, Morgan decided it was time to try for a central bank again. Using their combined financial muscle, Morgan and his friends were able to crash the stock market.
Thousands of small banks were vastly overextended. Some of Morgan's principal competitors went under. Some had reserves of less than one percent (1%), thanks to the fractional reserve banking technique.

Within days, runs on banks were commonplace across the nation. Now Morgan stepped into the public arena and offered to prop up the faltering American economy by supporting failing banks with money he generously offered to create out of nothing.

It was an outrageous proposal, worse than even fractional reserve banking, but, in a panic, Congress let him do it. Morgan manufactured $200 million worth of this completely reserveless, private money – and bought things with it, paid for services with it, and sent some of it to his branch banks to lend out at interest. His plan worked. Soon, the public regained confidence in money in general and quit hoarding their currency. But in the interim, many small banks failed and banking power was further consolidated into the hands of a few large banks. By 1908 the arranged panic was over and Morgan was hailed as a hero by the president of Princeton University, a naive man by the name of Woodrow Wilson, who naively wrote:

"All this trouble could be averted if we appointed a committee of six or seven public-spirited men like J.P. Morgan to handle the affairs of our country."

Economic textbooks would later explain that the creation of the Federal Reserve System was the direct result of the panic of 1907, quote: "with its alarming epidemic of bank failures: the country was fed up once and for all with the anarchy of unstable private banking."

But Minnesota Congressman Charles A. Lindbergh, Sr., the father of the famous aviator, "Lucky Lindy," later explained that the Panic of 1907 was really just a scam:

The Money Trust caused the 1907 panic... those not favorable to the
Money Trust could be squeezed out of business and the people
frightened into demanding changes in the banking and currency laws
which the Money Trust would frame."

Since the passage of the National Banking Act of 1863, the National Banks that Act established as a cartel, had been able to coordinate a series of booms and busts. The purpose was not only to fleece the American public of their property, but later to claim that the decentralized banking system was basically so unstable that it had to be further consolidated and control centralized into a central bank once again, as it had been before Jackson ended it.

The supremely critical economic issue of private vs. state ownership and control was carefully skirted, as was the fractional reserve banking fraud causing the booms and busts.

LEGAL DEFENSE AND DEFINITIONS:
Any Agent, Officer, Or Judge Against You, Demand Their Oath Of Office
We always begin our legal foundation with a demand that ALL government agents including officers, judges etc., who have touched the case or a part of your case in any way, produce certified copies of their
requisite oaths of office before any case is tried against you, transmitted via U.S. Mail (VERY IMPORTANT).
For state government officials, these oaths are required by federal law
(4 U.S.C. 101).
Thus, you can eventually remove your case into the DCUS, on the federal question that arises from their failure to produce a valid oath of office.
So, as part of your demand for their oaths of office, include also a demand that they exhibit the exact provisions of the U.S. Constitution which they have agreed to support. Couple this strategy with all other relief which you need, e.g. temporary injunction pending discovery of valid oaths of office.
A 30-day deadline is reasonable, beyond which you can invoke the Tweel fraud doctrine, and the Carmine estoppel doctrine. In this particular instance, the estoppel doctrine will give you a basis for striking from the court record, any and all oaths which are proffered AFTER your resonable deadline.
Striking them from the record is tantamount to showing that they DO NOT EXIST!
Also, all uncertified documents are inadmissible.
Couple this oath strategy with a demand that these government "actors" produce all competent waivers of your fundamental Right to due process of law, pursuant to the Fifth Amendment. You will know if you ever waived such an important Right. You very probably have NOT DONE SO!
"Waivers of fundamental rights must be knowingly intelligent acts, done with sufficient awareness of the relevant circumstances and likely consequences."
Brady v. U.S.
Finally, read the Universal Declaration of Human Rights, and the International Covenant on Civil and Political Rights, for a ton of important laws rendered

supreme Law by the Supremacy Clause in the U.S. Constitution.
Under the Privacy Act, 1974, Section 7:
(a)(1) It shall be unlawful for any Federal, State or local government agency to deny to any individual any right, benefit, or privilege provided by law because of such individual refusal to disclose his or her social security number. Pub, L.93-579, Section 7;5 U.S.C. Sec. 552a.
Note: unless (2) Disclosure is required by federal statute for welfare recipients to obtain and provide SSNs of children.
.

Section (b) Any Federal, State or local government Agency which requests an individual to disclose his social security account number shall inform that individual whether that disclosure is mandatory or voluntary, by what statutory or other authority such number is solicited, and what uses will be made of it.
"Right of privacy is a personal right designed to protect a person from unwanted disclosure of personal information." CNA Financial Corporation v Local 743, 515 F. Supp.942
.

Under 42USC 408, it is a Felony to use threat, duress, or coercion to try to force a person by fear or deceit to provide a SSN.
Defense Against Officers
The Police Officer swears by Oath to uphold the United States Constitution as an Officer Of Law. Supreme Court Decisions are Considered the Law of the Land In Regards to Constitutionally Protected Rights, and they cannot be interpreted, or reinterpreted,
as they are 'stare decisis' (already reviewed and clearly described as Law).
.

SUPREME COURT CASE:.
Kolender v. Lawson (461 U.S. 352, 1983) in which the United States Supreme Court ruled that a police officer could not arrest a citizen merely for refusing to present identification.
There is no such thing as
"Failure to identify"
YOU CAN SUE THE POLICE
FOR AN ILLEGAL ARREST AND
RESIST ARREST WITH IMPUNITY!

.

"An illegal arrest is an assault and battery. The person so attempted to be restrained of his liberty has the same right to use force in defending himself as he would in repelling any other assault and battery."
(State v. Robinson, 145 ME. 77, 72 ATL. 260).
"Each person has the right to resist an unlawful arrest. In such a case, the person attempting the arrest stands in the position of a wrongdoer and may be resisted by the use of force, as in selfdefense."
(State v. Mobley, 240 N.C. 476, 83 S.E. 2d 100).
"One may come to the aid of another being unlawfully arrested, just as he may where one is being assaulted, molested, raped or kidnapped. Thus it is not an offense to liberate one from the unlawful custody of an officer, even though he may have submitted to such custody, without resistance."
(Adams v. State, 121 Ga. 16, 48 S.E. 910).

"These principles apply as well to an officer attempting to make an arrest, who abuses his authority and transcends the bounds thereof by the use of unnecessary force and violence, as they do to a private individual who unlawfully uses such force and violence."
Jones v. State, 26 Tex. App. I; Beaverts v. State, 4 Tex. App. 1 75; Skidmore v. State, 43 Tex. 93, 903.
Police Officers can only ask for your identification when an investigation is under way. and you are a part of it. Therefore, when they hinder you, they are saying that
you are under investigation. Their car lights and sirens are to only go on if there is an investigation. Therefore they must identify to you the investigation, and your part in it. This is why you ask them "What is their probable cause".
ILLEGAL SEARCH: If they ask do you mind if they search the car? -- Say NO, you cannot search without a search warrant. If you pay attention, they always ask if you mind. They know they have to get your consent. Usually people agree to the search out of fear, or from the fact that they see them as the authority. However, they are with bounds, limits, and protocols, because they are for the purpose of upholding the law, keeping the peace, protecting the citizens, and preserving the rights of the people.
YOU CAN NOT HAVE A TRIAL WITHOUT AN INJURED PARTY

You cannot, as a matter of Due Process of Law even be called or summons into a Court or Tribunal without having an INJURED PARTY. The injured party is the Accuser and he or she must squarely and surely identify you as the Accused. The accused (you) has either committed an injury to a body (corpus delecti) or injured property or have breached a contract. If so, then the accuser (injuired party) must be present and the contract must also be placed as evidence for review. The Accuser (injured party) must put the judicial machinery into action by FIRST writing a sworn affidavit that states the injuries that were committed. Then the summons comes and it must be signed by an Article III judge, which states that the matter has been duly investigated and probable cause for such summons and / or warrant is justified. (See Amendment IV). These are all matters of Due Process of Law and if one of these elements are missing and or corrupted in anyway , the entire matter must be dismissed.

Be sure you are able to "keep a circle around your passions and square your conduct". The following case law states that you can use deadly force against public servants, including law enforcement officers, who unlawfuly enter your home or your personal body. This includes entrance without a lawful warrant. A lawful warrant must have a complainant's (injured party) sworn affidavit attached to it and it must be signed with a raised seal by an Article III Judge, as that is the ONLY Judge. Magistrates of ministerial and administrative courts are not judges. This then, puts a different light on those DYFS or family service agencies and agents who come to your home feigning as government (Public Officials) and as if they have authority over you. Maybe that is why in some instances they come with a SWAT team to take your children, which is kidnapping in every sense of the word, as they have no jurisdictional authority to come in the first place. Police are agents and police departments are an agency, and they are NOT a government agency, therefore their actions must be within the bounds of Law, they are not to violate the rights of the people or they can be held accountable and you can protect another citizen if you witness them (policemen) using excessive force or otherwise violating the rights of another.

The Birth Certificate is an instrument of 'human trafficking'. It is adminstered from a private agency, although many think it is the government - it is NOT!! It is the foreign corporate state that colludes with the Hospitals to create a certificate of each child born and then turn it over to the corporate state for them to record as public record under their jurisdiction. Any instruments administered from a corporation places you under the jurisdiction of a corporation and thereby identifies you as a corporation, or property of a corporation (chattel). The highest form of identification is the footprint or thumbprint. This is why they utilize a 'footprint' on the birth certificate for your child. They stamp it onto the certificate created and established under the jurisdiction of a corporation, which makes your child a corporation at birth. Thus - 'human trafficking'. Therefrom they deny your child's rights of birth and violate your liberties and their liberties. It is all done in a methodical manner which misleads the unsuspecting and unknowing natural people into believing they must have a birth certificate, when they do not, a birth record can be established, however a birth certificate absolutely implies an exchange, as in a 'Bill of Exchange'

THE METAPHYSIC SOCIETY ASSOCIATION
Dr.Osei Kufuor